THE

BLACK

CANOE

THE BLACK CANOE

BILL REID AND THE SPIRIT OF HAIDA GWAII

Text: Robert Bringhurst
Photographs: Ulli Steltzer

DOUGLAS & McINTYRE, VANCOUVER/TORONTO

Douglas & McIntyre Ltd.
1615 Venables Street
Vancouver, British Columbia
V5L 2H1

Published with assistance from the British
Columbia Heritage Trust.

The excerpt from ''Old Timers'' in
Cornhuskers by Carl Sandburg, copy-
right 1918 by Holt, Rinehart and
Winston, Inc. and renewed 1946 by Carl
Sandburg, is reprinted by permission of
Harcourt Brace Jovanovich, Inc.

Printed and bound in Singapore.

92 93 94 95 96 5 4 3 2 1

*Canadian Cataloguing in Publication
Data*:

Bringhurst, Robert, 1946–
    The black canoe

    Includes bibliographical references.
    ISBN 1-55054-037-8
    1. Reid, Bill, 1920–   Spirit of
Haida Gwaii.   2. Haida Indians –
Religion and mythology.   3. Haida
Indians – Sculpture   4. Indians of
North America – Northwest Coast of
North America – Religion and
mythology.   5. Indians of North
America – Northwest Coast of North
America – Sculpture.
    I. Steltzer, Ulli, 1923–
    II. Title.
    NB249.R43A77 1992   730'.92
    C92-091111-0

CONTENTS

Aagwa naanang tlagaaguut
diinang kwiindalani.
Waghan sttagha kujawaanii.
Gam hla kunggingang ang.

In his grandmother's land
my child is striding.
Therefore his foot is precious.
Don't keep crying.

  – Cradle song of the Hl'yaalangkunlnagai

Once out of nature I shall never take
My bodily form from any natural thing,
But such a form as Grecian goldsmiths make
Of hammered gold and gold enamelling
To keep a drowsy Emperor awake;
Or set upon a golden bough to sing
To lords and ladies of Byzantium
Of what is past, or passing, or to come.

  – William Butler Yeats, "Sailing to Byzantium"

PROLOGUE

THE SUBJECT of this book is the meaning of a single piece of sculpture. The search for that meaning reaches out and back through history, literature, politics, biology and other distant lands. Meaning ends where it begins, yet it refuses to be confined. The sculpture sits on Pennsylvania Avenue in Washington, DC, and it portrays an instantly familiar, age-old image: travellers in a boat. Yet the identity and nature of those travellers, the location of the sculpture — in the chancery courtyard of Canada's embassy to the USA — and even its name, *The Spirit of Haida Gwaii*, pose complicated questions. Ulli Steltzer began to photograph the work in 1986, when it existed only in embryo, as a protean clay sketch. The words in this book, like the photographs, are largely concerned with submerged or hidden aspects of the sculpture: with truths that never were, or are no longer, visible to the naked eye.

Earlier generations of Haida called their archipelago *Xhaaidlagha Gwaayaai* or *Xhaaidla Gwaayaai*, The Islands at the Boundary of the World. The shorter form, *Haida Gwaii*, which means The Islands of the People, is recent coinage, though the connection it names between the people and the place is ancient fact. This shortened form of the name has also been officially adopted by the Council of the Haida Nation and now is widely used.

See the Note on Interpretations and Sources, page 161.

If culture were language — which to a large extent it is — Haida culture of the present day might also merit a different name from Haida culture of two centuries ago. The terminology would acknowledge a cultural sea-change, like the shift from Anglo-Saxon and Gaelic to English, from Latin to Italian, from Egyptian and Phoenician and the other ancient tongues of the Middle East to the Arabic that prevails there today — or indeed, like the shift from the Haida language to English, which prevails today in Haida Gwaii.

But culture is not only language, and names alone give an inaccurate picture of change and continuity either way. Much as it has altered during two bitter centuries of religious and mercantile pressure — and again in twenty years of unequal and unopposite but conscious reaction to that pressure — life in Haida Gwaii remains in many ways its own. Assimilation, like segregation, has failed.

Beneath the art, the politics, the history, lie other, deeper worlds: the land, the sea, the creatures that inhabit them — and an answering web of interlocking stories. The mutable, delicate, self-repairing tissue of Haida mythology, like the forests and streams, beaches and reefs it was born in, has been heavily mistreated for many decades; like the land and water, it is nevertheless alive.

Much of this world persists in concentrated silence, like the forest in its seeds. Its monuments are scattered from Skidegate to London, Ottawa to Leningrad, Vancouver to New York. Yet the dignity, intelligence and hospitality of this mythworld persevere. Anyone willing to watch and listen is privileged to encounter both the resilient, adaptable creatures of Haida mythology and, keeping their company, some equally remarkable human beings.

There are the carvers, living and dead, though we have names, dates and faces now for relatively few of them, like Charles Edenshaw and Bill Reid. For some we have conjectural identities and tags, such as the Master of the Black Field, the Master of the Long Fingers, the Master of the Chicago Settee. The rest are more anonymous: invisible hands and minds whose thought lives purely in their works, seldom disturbed by interpretations and uncontaminated even by the most conjectural biographies and names.

Behind them stand the old oral poets of Haida Gwaii. Storytellers, like carvers, are still to be found in the islands, but the narratives and visions of the early masters survive in far fewer numbers than the early paintings and carvings. Those that have crossed the boundary into written language take the form of silent, halting transcriptions, yet they inform and sustain the works of the visual artists even now. Two of these mythtellers – Walter McGregor of the Qaayahllaanas and John Sky of the Qquuna Qiighawaai – who were contemporaries of Tolstoy and Johannes Brahms, seem to me also to merit some of their fame. I regard them as among the greatest poets of the Western Hemisphere whose words have been preserved.

The art of the early storytellers and carvers comes to us now through the intervention of strangers – the quiet listener John Swanton, who transcribed the words of those Haida poets nearly a century ago; and a number of scientists, traders, thieves and casual buyers who shipped their loot to museums and private hoards around the world. Nor should we forget, on this occasion, the photographers – George Dawson, Edward Dossetter, C.F. Newcombe, Edward Curtis, and the improbable Hannah Maynard – whose sometimes crisp but often faint glass negatives, made at the close of the nineteenth century, are the only surviving record of many works of Haida sculpture. Haida Gwaii is not the only nation whose greatest treasures of art and thought have passed indifferently, like money, through noble and venal, reverent and predatory hands.

I use the words myth and mythology often in this book, never in the modern sense of a perpetuated lie, but in the older sense of an inescapable truth: one that insistently reappears in narrative form. Myths are stories that reach outside of human time. Saloustios, who was theological counsellor to Julian the Apostate, the throwback pagan emperor of Constantinople and Rome in the fourth century A D, defended the myths of his tribal forebears as meaningful fictions. "These things never happened," Saloustios writes, "but they always *are*."

At home in their own world, the myths not only are, they also happen. Day by day they reoccur, fuse, split, contract in the face of cynical hostility and expand to absorb new information. It is not continued telling that makes them real, but their continuing reality that leads them to be told.

The grudging label of meaningful fiction may nevertheless be the best that Rome and Washington can offer them. Whatever myths they are – Christ's vision in the desert, Moses' vision on the mountain, Aphrodite's birth in the seafoam from the severed balls of her father, or the Raven's theft and dispersal of light and salmon – when they actually happen, they do so out-of-doors, in dreams, in darkness: where human beings perceive themselves as vital but minor participants in the world.

In the context of the myths told by the poets of Haida Gwaii, I also speak of gods. I have chosen the word deliberately, hoping to summon some of its earlier and least pretentious meanings. The gods, or spirits of place, or resident powers, of Haida myth are older than writing, older than empire, older than the city, the priest, the temple, the garden, the farm. Their counterparts in Europe survived the reign of Olympian Zeus in the guise of rural deities – nereids, nymphs, river gods, winds and other creatures, chthonic, atmospheric and especially marine. In Asia, Confucian and Hindu and Buddhist regimes have sometimes left the local spirits similar room. Christianity on the whole has been less merciful, degrading them to the sprites, fairies, leprechauns and elves of European children's tales.

Haida oral literature tells us that the powers living around and within the Islands were honored, respected and fed – by placing calcined shells, tobacco and other gifts into the fire or passing them through the skin of the sea on a paddle blade. Nothing whatsoever suggests that these beings were worshipped. Here I call them gods in an effort to acknowledge both their nature and their power, and not because I mistake them for anthropomorphic projections or objects of worship or abstract ideas. Nor do I understand them to have any preferential contract with the human species. In Haida myth, while the gods are fully capable of taking human form, their archetypal incarnation is the killer whale.

"Our welfare involves something beyond us," Aristotle says, "but a god is his own well-being." John Sky of the Qquuna Qiighawaai and

Eudemian Ethics *1245b18*

9

Walter of the Qaayahllaanas would, I think, have questioned the second half of this statement. The world of their stories is one in which reciprocal relations are always involved. The gods and heroes they name, though superhuman, are not omnipotent. Least of all are they immune to the cycle of death and rebirth or to other ecological rules. They are the embodiment of the knowledge that the land and the sea are sustainable but mortal, intelligent but changeable, continuous but plural, and in short, intensely alive. The habit of calling them supernatural — established by John Swanton almost a century ago — therefore seems to me misleading.

This subject is taken up again in more technical terms on page 162f.

*

Now as in the old days, when a totem pole is carved in Haida Gwaii, the carving is generally done in public view. Speeches are made when the pole is raised, stories are told, and a feast is given. In what is still primarily an oral culture, these events will fuel further stories, which will centre on the pole. No less than the Trajan Column, the pole becomes the record of its own occasion: a monument where history and myth lay claim to one another and where the spoken word and visual image are joined. In the headlong and triumphal outer world, where memory and community lean heavily on printed texts and photographs, few works of sculpture are publicly embraced in such a way. Few become the central subjects of books; still fewer do so from the moment they are installed. But most works of representational sculpture in the dominant traditions, if they reach beyond political assertiveness and personal ambition — all the Moseses and Christs and Davids, Virgins and Laocoöns — are works for which the books have already been written.

"Tolerance," writes Claude Lévi-Strauss, "is not a contemplative position, the dispensing of indulgence to what was and to what is. It is a dynamic attitude consisting in foresight, understanding and encouragement of that which wants to be."

See "Race et histoire," Anthropologie structurale II, 1973. This essay first appeared in the UNESCO anthology La Question raciale devant la science moderne, Paris, 1952.

I could be wrong, but I have the impression that what wants to be in Canada at present is a complex multiplicity of things, not all of which are provided for or dreamt of in colonial and immigrant institutions and traditions. I have tried to trace a single one of the threads, one of the voices, in this inconclusive, polylingual music — one which begins with the creation of the world in a North Pacific archipelago and fetches up for now on the Atlantic, mindful of the ease with which such worlds have been damaged and destroyed. From beginning to end, that thread insists on its own integrity, all the while linking many things. Like a weaver's yarn or a sailor's line, it is made of many strands in its turn.

A few years' study of the languages, oral literature and visual art of the Northwest Coast of North America has made me no authority on a heritage in which I was not raised. Still less has it made me an expert on the customs and beliefs of the Haida people. On these subjects, the Haida are of course their own best spokesmen. I have left out much that is important to those now living in the Islands, ironically enough, while trying to elucidate, for others, some of the meanings of a sculpture called *The Spirit of Haida Gwaii.*

I did not wish to write an official and approved interpretation of the sculpture – or of the history, the myths, and the political aspirations it calls to mind. There is room in this case for several official views – that of the Haida, that of the government of Canada, and that of the artist, Bill Reid, all three of whom are eminently capable of speaking for themselves. But official views, like official portraits, are in my experience usually falsifications, and I am certain that in this case there are really many different points of view on every side. At least a few of them coexist here in the pages of this book, along with the many points of view in Ulli Steltzer's consummate photographs.

I

SURROUNDED by dressed limestone, steel, aluminum, reinforced concrete, bulletproof glass, and the sounds of government limousines, tour buses, trucks and private automobiles, a black canoe sits motionless in the water. Like a lifeboat, it is filled to overflowing. Some of its passengers are incongruously serene, others intent, still others jumpy or distraught. A man in formal dress stands imperturbably amidships. But this vessel's living cargo consists of more than human beings. There are birds, bears, a frog and other animals, some on watch and the others urgently paddling. A raven the size of a grizzly is steering. The beaver is gritting his buck teeth; the eagle is biting the bear's paw; the wolf has his fangs in the eagle's wing. Yet for all their activity, these figures are now as motionless as the canoe: caught in mid-stroke by the black bronze, while the water — so long as the pumps work — skirls beneath them.

Few stories are older or more widespread than that of the great flood. And the ecological metaphor of a lifeboat crowded with mammals, birds and amphibians is difficult to miss, like the realization that there is nowhere to escape to. This ark is not a spaceship; it is earth- and seabound: an ancient and sophisticated mating of organic grace and patience with technological audacity and skill. It is an ocean-going canoe: a steerable leaf, coaxed stroke by stroke by hand from the grain of a prehistoric tree, propelled now stroke by stroke through shifting wind and current into whatever future still remains.

But to understand this vessel and its cargo, we must also go a shorter and more painful distance back. We must regress two hundred years, to another wooden vessel, emerging under sail out of the mists of the North Pacific, making landfall at an archipelago known then to its inhabitants as the Islands at the Boundary of the World and now as the Islands of the People, Haida Gwaii. That moving ship, like this motionless black canoe, stitched timelessness to time.

By the Christian calendar, it was 1787. The ship was a British merchant vessel, the *Queen Charlotte*. Her captain, not enquiring how the people he met and the world he had suddenly entered chose to be named, called the archipelago after the vessel in which he arrived. On charts and maps drawn by people who have never been there, or by those who have not stayed long enough, it is shown even now as the Queen Charlotte Islands. And though no treaty was ever signed with its inhabitants, it has been mapped since 1871 as part of Canada. Hecate Strait — a hundred miles of shallow water, treacherous in the frequent storms — lies between the Islands and the Tsimshian coast of the British Columbia mainland. On the west, the bottom drops abruptly to a thousand fathoms, and the blue swells fetch from Sakhalin and Japan.

The *Queen Charlotte* was not the first European craft sighted by the Haida. A Spanish vessel had called briefly at the northern end of the archipelago in 1774, and a British ship in 1786 at the southern end. Russian traders had also made their first commercial assaults on southeastern Alaska, not far away. That news and a few trade goods from the industrializing world had certainly come to Haida Gwaii through the long-established routes of aboriginal trade. Fishing junks from China and Japan, and canoes from Hawaii, had probably crossed, deliberately or otherwise, at unknown dates, and with or without a living crew on board when they arrived. But the *Queen Charlotte* was the first intruding vessel to undertake extensive and direct trade with the Haida. She circumnavigated the Islands, buying furs, and at the end of that first season, she bore away in her hold some two thousand sea otter skins to be sold in the dockside markets of Macao.

News of the rich new trading frontier spread through the merchant fleets in the Pacific, and the Islands were visited by other traders. Half a century later, the sea otter of Haida Gwaii were effectively extinct. Marten was next on the fur traders' list; then land otter and black bear. Whaling fleets gathered annually in the Islands during the later nineteenth century. A land-based whaling station, a dogfish oil works and salmon canneries were built. Miners came for the gold and other minerals, loggers for the timber. Species by species and watershed by watershed, the richest layers and corners of the Haida world were looted for export, and the looters with few exceptions then moved on.

When the *Queen Charlotte* sailed into Haida waters, at the end of the eighteenth century, the Islands were home to a wealthy and settled culture of mesolithic seahunters. Their language, which in the 1990s is closer to extinction than the whooping crane, bore no obvious relationship to any other spoken anywhere on earth. But their mythology, their oral literature, their music and dance and visual art were intimately linked with those of the Tlingit, the Tsimshian, Gitksan and Nishga, and the Heiltsuk, Haisla and Nuxalk, who populate the rest of the coast of northern British Columbia and southeastern Alaska. The archaeological record suggests that this pattern of life had developed in situ without radical change over some 2500 to 3000 years, but the record of human habitation in the Islands extends at least 5000 years beyond that. Still earlier sites are likely to exist, though they will now be under water — flooded by the rising seas that followed the last ice age.

The Haida of earlier days built large rectangular houses — massive post-and-beam frames of the durable, fragrant wood of redcedar, finished with redcedar slabs for the low-pitched roof, adzed planks for the walls, and adzed or relief-carved planks lining the stepped sides of the large, rectangular sunken galleries that surrounded the central fire. Each house that asserted its standing in the community did so by means of a wooden spire, the frontal pole, on which the artists of the Northern Coast carved the figures of their mythology and matrilinear heraldry. Totems, the Europeans liked to call them — disguising the fact that their significance was in principle not so different from that of the images of the garden, annunciation and crucifixion in European homes and churches, and the rampant lions, scallop shells and lilies of European coats-of-arms. They proclaimed the sacred stories of the creation and arrangement of the world, and the social rights and obligations asserted by the families who made that world their home.

Mortuary poles, holding remains of the dead aloft in their coffins, and memorial poles for members of the family whose bodies rested elsewhere, stood to either side of the door in front of the houses. Heraldic figures were painted and carved into these poles also, and often into the shorter internal houseposts. On the beach in front of the poles lay the canoes, ranging up to twenty metres, carved and steamed from single logs of redcedar. Canoes were also sometimes painted stem and stern with the abstracted, stylized forms of crest animals. Particular favorites, at least in the nineteenth century, included large carnivores, such as the wolf and killer whale.

Hunting bows were of yew, halibut hooks and fishing spears of alder barbed with ivory or bone. Woodworking tools and household implements were of stone, bone, shell, maple, alder, mountain goat horn, walrus ivory and baleen. Rain hats were woven of split and peeled spruce root. Capes were woven of pounded redcedar bark — a substance which in a skilled woman's hands becomes as soft as vicuna or lamb's wool, and more waterproof and long-wearing. Bedding was of bearskin and other furs over cushions of moss. Storage chests were of redcedar, yellowcedar and alder. Bowls and spoons were of alder and mountain sheep horn. These hats, chests, spoons, bowls, halibut hooks, fish clubs, and other tools were likewise often painstakingly painted with brushes of porcupine hair, and carved with beavertooth chisels, musselshell adzes and cold-hammered trade-metal blades.

Then as now, the Haida diet consisted of salmon, halibut, snapper, cod, clams, cockles, mussels, crab and other fish and shellfish; sea slugs and sea urchin roe; the oil of eulachon and black bear; the flesh of sea lion, seal and other mammals of the sea and land. Wild fruit — huckleberry, blueberry, bearberry, strawberry, salmonberry, cranberry, wild apple, cherry — was gathered and dried in season, like the salmon. Ducks and geese were hunted. Wild vegetables were harvested from the sea and from the land. The rootstocks and fiddleheads of ferns, and the nutritious inner bark of western hemlock and shore pine were eaten. Early traders brought the potato, but myth and archaeology concur that in the older Haida world there was but one semidomesticated plant: a now-vanished species of tobacco.

For ornament, the Haida and their neighbors had jewelry of carved bone, raw copper, dentalium shell, and the claws of grizzly and black bear. Their fine-dress garments were of sea otter and marten fur. Their dancing blankets were tapestries: the abstract, symmetrical forms of animals, finger-woven of mountain goat hair and the long, supple fibres of the bark of yellowcedar. In these habitable maps of animal power, all the organs and inherent spirits of the body come to the surface of the skin as stylized eyes and ears and faces.

Ceremonial headdresses and masks — more eyes and ears and faces — were carved from redcedar and alder, garnished with eagle down, sea lion whiskers, human hair, ermine pelts and mallard skin, inlaid with chips of abalone shell and the ivory-like opercula of red-turban sea snails. In addition to this finery, the people wore the feathers of red-breasted sapsuckers, northern flickers, western tanagers, peregrine falcons, Steller's jays.

For their day-to-day clothing, shelter and transportation, the Haida depended profoundly on a single species of tree, the western redcedar, which pollen samples tell us has been plentiful in the Islands for 5000 years. But the Haida were fishing people and seahunters. Their art, their mythology, their sense of life and death and of meaning and symbol — their daily intellectual sustenance — came, like their food, almost wholly from animal sources. There are tales of Haida princes arriving at feasts wearing necklaces of live frogs, and their wives with live rufous hummingbirds tied to their hair, where the more horticultural peoples of Polynesia and Central America might have worn flowers.

Like the Inuit, Eyak and Aleut of the north coasts, the Yaghan of southern Chile and many other peoples around the Pacific, the Haida lived primarily at and on the surface of the sea: in boats and in the intertidal zone. They lived in intimate familiarity with that membrane, sometimes savage, sometimes calm, through which grebes and harbor seals and killer whales, harpoons and halibut lines and paddles vanish, refract and reappear. This membrane, called *xhaaidla* in Haida, stretches skin-tight and resonant over everything in the world of Haida myth. It is the surface of the sea, the land, the sky: the skin of the world, through which the black bears pass as they enter their dens, the killer whales as they sound, and the sharp-shin hawks and eagles as they glide behind the mountain. When they cross that boundary and enter their houses, the mythtellers say, the animals take off their feather cloaks or skins. There they appear to one another, and converse with one another, just as we do here among ourselves. They too, in other words, are people. Haida poets say the gods call human beings *xhaaidla xhitiit giidai,* "common surface birds," because we need animal escorts, nonhuman powers or guides, in order to penetrate that skin between the world we can see and the ones we dream of, sing of, paint and carve. But the usual name for us wingless, finless, gill-less, naked creatures is simply surface people, *xhaaidla xhaaidaghai,* as distinct from the people of the forest, sky and sea: *hlkkyaan isgyan sagwa isgyan taangghwan xhaaidaghai.*

Digging for clams and setting for halibut, the Haida grew used to hunting for and finding what they could not see. They learned, as fishermen do, to read the water, and as hunters do, to read in their dreams the movements of game. They learned to read the three- and four-dimensional world of ocean, beach and salmon stream through signs in two dimensions or in low relief. A similar sense of hidden wealth and contained vitality developed in their art. The world of classical Haida painting and sculpture is a living, breathing, fertile world beneath a skin of organic abstraction, a world of sensuous surprise behind the screen of formal order, and a world of nourishing ideas behind a surface of tense stillness, compressed to two, or little more than two, dimensions.

The range of skill and talent evident in surviving pieces of traditional Haida art, and the known practice of the nineteenth-century carvers, seems to confirm that before the coming of the Europeans, painting and sculpture in Haida Gwaii were a routine part of male adult life as well as a specialized calling for recognized masters of the craft. Though some excelled at it, everyone learned the visual language, just as everyone learned to speak – and for good reason. That refined visual style and animal iconography was the nearest thing to writing the Haida had. It was how they reminded themselves of what they knew, and one another of what they believed.

For several decades after Europeans discovered the place, the visual art of the Haida and neighboring cultures flared with exhilarating brightness. The primary reasons were the sudden injection of wealth – which the Haida chose to spend in large amounts by commissioning art from those who were most skilled – and the equally sudden injection of new technology, in the form of metal tools. A secondary reason was the new cross-cultural market for souvenirs. Perhaps for the first time on the Northwest Coast, there arose a fully professional artist class. But while this brief light burned, the silence gathered, and the intellectual and artistic world of the Haida rapidly decayed.

Haida society as Europeans first encountered it was divided into two sides or moieties – *qqwal* in Haida – called the Eagle side and the Raven side. Marriage to a member of the same side, no matter the presence or absence of blood relationship as Europeans conceive it, was regarded as incest. As easy and frequent as death, marriage was also of cosmic importance, like finding one's own reflection or counterpart on the other side of the *xhaaidla*: it reunited the two sides.

Each side consisted in turn of several dozen families or clans (*gwaigyaghang*) with names such as Qaayahllaanas (Sea Lion People) and Naikun Qiighawaai (Those Born at House Point), each sharing in the general body of Haida mythology and each with a tributary narrative tradition of its own. These families, like the villages and individual households, were typically headed by men, but inheritance of physical goods, position, intellectual property and privileges, including titles, names, songs and the guardianship of certain stories, was through the female line. Children both male and female belonged to the lineage of their mother. Male children were therefore groomed to succeed their maternal uncles, who always belonged to their own side, instead of their fathers, who always belonged to the opposite side. And succession, as well as merit, was of great importance. It was a hierarchical culture, with *kilstl* (spokesmen or exemplars) and *iittlgha* (owners or guardians, both male and female) at the top, and at the bottom a class of humans treated as chattels: *xhaldaang jidaai* (captives or slaves).

Many and deep as the differences were, Haida society at the moment of European contact was in several respects like the one that engulfed it. It was already wealthy, and it was eager to be more so: open to the ravages of materialism, pride and social ambition. It was not utopia, nor wilderness, nor a state of noble savagery. And it was not what Europeans have preferred to call it: a New World. Haida culture, with its foibles, cruelties, beauties, profundities and peculiarities, had been thousands of years in the making.

Had the Haida been perfectly content with their lives as they were, they might have refused altogether to trade with the Europeans – though in that case, force would soon have been applied. As it was, the Haida coveted some of the European trade goods, particularly metal, just as the Europeans – who had hunted most of their own large mammals to extinction – envied the animal wealth of the Haida world. The Haida bought knives, hatchets, cooking pots, jewelry, and scrap from which to make weapons and tools to their own design. Thereby they became, for a time, still more efficient hunters and craftsmen. Then came firearms and ammunition – which made them, in the short term, more efficient still, but placed between them and their world a barrier of power expensive to sustain and very difficult to cross. Soon, through the Hudson's Bay Company posts, came the consumer goods that distanced them further from the living, immediate world, and from the world of their art and

Many cultures other than the Haida balance and tighten the social fabric by emphasizing cross-relations – male relations on the mother's side and female relations on the father's. Even the early Romans did so. That is why a mother's brother (qaa in Haida) is called in Latin avunculus (*the diminutive or affectionate form of* avus, *which means grandfather or ancestor), while a father's brother is* patruus. *And a father's sister (sqaan in Haida) is in Latin* amita, *close friend, while a mother's sister is* matertera, *another mother. A man's important female relatives in the world of Haida myth – apart from mother, grandmother, sister and wife – are* l sqaangha, *his paternal aunt, and* l qaagha jaagha daughanaagas, *his mother's youngest brother's wife.*

traditional culture: glazed windows, factory crockery, cotton cloth and readymade clothing, trade tobacco, rum, sugar, molasses, flour and tea, door hinges, padlocks and hasps, and the *Illustrated London News* to keep them abreast of imperial fashion.

Greed and insatiability are phenomena contemplated at length in Haida mythology. But the eighteenth-century Haida, like other un-colonized peoples, had no practical experience in dealing with unlimited demand. If the wisdom of the myths was understood by some, it was clearly misunderstood or ignored by many others, among the Haida just as among the Europeans – who have, after all, myths of the same kind. Like other peoples suddenly touched by the power and brilliance of empire – and perhaps more eagerly than most – the Haida joined in their own transformation. But in their case, the forces of commerce were soon overtaken by an even more potent agent of change.

At the beginning of the nineteenth century, the native population of Haida Gwaii was probably close to 7000, living in thirty or forty communities along the 6000 or more ragged kilometres of coastline that surround and feed the Islands. Some 2000 additional Haida lived in a half dozen newer island villages at the southern tip of Alaska.

By the end of the same century, a series of smallpox epidemics had reduced the total population to less than one thousand, and the number of inhabited villages in Haida Gwaii had fallen to its present number: two. By 1911, the Alaskan Haida community had been reduced to two villages as well.

While there is no question that this holocaust as a whole was unpremeditated, there is also no question that it was real, and that it was brought upon the Haida by the intrusion of the Europeans. There is evidence also of several occasions on which a known carrier of the disease was deliberately set ashore among the native population. In absolute number of deaths, the near extinction of the Haida, who were never a large nation, ranks far down the list of modern disasters. And there are many Native American nations, like the Huron of Ontario, the Beothuk of Newfoundland, the Kumivit, Chumash and Yahi of California, and the Bororo of Brazil, who fared still worse. But the Haida experience remains, on its modest scale, a very convincing demonstration of the horrors of biological warfare.

Fishermen and weavers, children and grandmothers, carvers and storytellers died. Families and villages disintegrated. The survivors gathered in Skidegate, Masset and Hydaburg – the three communities served by Christian missionaries – and in the smaller Alaskan cannery town of New Kasaan. Then came the government assimilation programs. Haida children, like those from other native nations of the Northwest Coast, were forced into boarding schools, where they were forbidden to speak their own languages, to maintain the traditional

According to Haida oral tradition, the Alaskan Haida villages were first colonized from the town of Daadans, in northeastern Haida Gwaii. The date of this migration has not been established, but it may have been as late as 1750.

19

Tanu, Haida Gwaii. July 1878. The town at this date consisted of about two dozen houses. Only seven are visible in this photograph. At least a dozen canoes can be seen on the beach. Eight housepoles, eight mortuary poles (some of them partially obscured) and three memorial poles are visible as well. At the head of the beach, a carver is at work on a new housepole. A small group of visitors is clustered around the memorial pole in front of the second house from the left. All but one of the canoes are positioned in the normal manner, stern to the village, bow to the sea, ready for launching. *Photo by George Dawson. National Archives of Canada, National Photography Collection,* PA 37753.

21

proprieties of moiety separation and clan distinction, and as a rule even to draw, carve and paint in the native forms. Their elders, during the same years, risked imprisonment for celebrating traditional ceremonies required for naming, marriage, funerals, the assumption of office and the exculpation of shame. The law that forbade native Canadians to perform the central rituals of their culture remained in force for more than sixty years, lapsing only in 1951. What remained of traditional Haida culture, after the population had shrunk by a factor of ten, was substantially curtailed by this means.

Once, before history came with its lethal gifts to Haida Gwaii, there was scarcely a stream or a reef or a cove, or a species of fish or mammal or bird, that lacked its place in the multidimensional mythological web, the narrative map of relations between the Haida and their world. Even now, abused as it is, the land is thick with images and stories, rich with meanings beyond the reach of history. But the mythscape of the Islands – just as rich and intricate as the forests and the sea – was also every bit as fragile, and it was the first to be despoiled. The fur trade and the firearms, the smallpox epidemics, the missionaries and government schools, and the potlatch law of 1884, which forbade the ceremonials, were only the first assaults. In their wake came the commercial overfishing and the clearcut logging that continue even now, beneath the growing threat of oil spills, to take their toll of the land and its indigenous intelligence: the joint creation of trees, crustaceans, molluscs, amphibians, fish, cetaceans, fur-bearing mammals and human beings. In traditional Haida thought, pride of place in this complex world was given not to man and his machines but to killer whales and to a large, omnivorous, tricky, unmusical but articulate black bird.

In place of the ancient villages and the old tidewater culture, in which humans had a stable and dependent rather than managerial role, a national park has now been tentatively established in the southern quarter of Haida Gwaii. This too is one more event in a chain. The museum collections of Haida painting and sculpture, and John Swanton's collections of Haida oral literature, now nearly a century old, have also become in a manner of speaking the national parks of the Haida mind. Some venture there for a weekend of amusement or a week of restoration. Others – a few, like Bill Reid – have taken up spiritual and intellectual residence, in order to recreate themselves. Of those few, fewer still, like Reid, have found a means to share their potent rediscoveries. Potent enough that they may end up recreating the rest of us as well.

And that is a measure of Reid's importance. Whether one comes to his work from traditional Haida art or the art of the ubiquitous white world, it opens the door to an entire artistic and intellectual tradition.

II

THEIR KNOWLEDGE of the sea distinguished the peoples of the Northwest Coast from most other hunters and gatherers, but what set them most fully apart was their sense of home. The world's other hunting cultures – virtually all now extinguished or extensively transformed in the name of civilization – moved with the seasons and the game. They lived in portable or temporary houses – tipis, wickiups, igloos – or in the natural shelter of caves, carrying little more than their consummate knowledge and skill. The Haida too made seasonal voyages – to their fish camps for the salmon run, to the halibut grounds, to gather edible ferns, fruits and shellfish, and to trade, feast and quarrel with their neighbors – but these were normally short forays from fixed settlements. While the adventurers among them sometimes travelled far afield, the people as a whole took full advantage of their option to hunt and fish year round from a single base. The sea brought nearly everything they needed within easy reach – just as, in time, it brought them what they needed least of all.

Even the Magdalenian hunters, who engraved and painted the ceilings and walls of Lascaux and Altamira some 15,000 years ago, were migratory peoples. Their art, mating improvisatory gesture and lyrical simplicity with naturalistic precision, is all on small, portable artifacts or existing natural surfaces. The peoples of the Northwest Coast, whose works exude compactness, containment and bursting efflorescence, along with a love of formal symmetry, created their own structures and surfaces instead. They built houses, towns and monuments, and made and used material possessions, on a scale known elsewhere only to agricultural peoples.

They were builders, yet like migratory hunters, the Haida cherished the knowledge, the skill, the idea, more than its physical incarnation. For all the energy, wealth and skill they invested in large sculpture, they were content to create it of wood and leave it exposed in the North Pacific weather. Coffins and funerary monuments, also of wood, were left to weather as well. Immortality lay in the cyclic reincarnation of spirit and form, the inheritance and bequest of name and position, and the metabolic recirculation of flesh, not in the preservation of funerary monuments or the embalming of remains. The peoples of the Northwest Coast were hunters, not agriculturalists, in their attitude toward death and, one may say, toward taxes also. Nothing offended their European visitors more deeply than the Haidas' self-sustaining social economy, which centred on the potlatch. In most of the ceremonials and celebrations now gathered under this catch-all English name, accrued wealth in substantial amounts is given away; more rarely, objects of special value are deliberately destroyed. One of the side effects, of course, is that without any need of trading posts or tourists, dealers or collectors, and without unsustainable pressure on the ecology, new art objects, and the workmanship and insight they require, are in continuous high demand.

Aesthetically, the culture was self-sustaining as well. Reinvigoration was a value; change as such was not. Painter and sculptor, therefore, were more nearly interpretive artists than creators in the modern sense. Until the European invasion brought catastrophic changes to their world, Haida sculptors had comparatively little need to distinguish themselves by seeking new forms or perspectives. Their role was to execute known images, though certainly not without room in which to improvise and compose. Accomplished artists had their individual styles, which are still quite recognizable, and the informal genres allowed considerable room for topical expression. But within the scope of the formal art, the execution of visual images was closely bound by custom. Paintbrush and adze were central instruments less of private search than of public affirmation.

What survives of this art tradition now is a diaspora of carved and painted objects, weavings, transcriptions of oral literature, some belated still photographs, and a few reels of still more belated acoustic tape and film. Arising from that, we have the resuscitated knowledge and skill of Bill Reid and a modest number of younger artists. We know only in a superficial way how classical Haida visual art was integrated with music, the dance, ritual theatre and mime. On the evidence, there was such an integration, and the dance was central to it. Reid has remained primarily aloof from the ceremonial revival, but a number of younger Haida artists now devote substantial amounts of their energy to learning the old songs and making new ones, reinventing the dance, and painting and carving the wearable art that the dances require.

Taken as a whole, Northwest Coast visual art (and the oral literature also) embraces most of the spectrum from close realism to rigorous abstraction. It includes, at one extreme, a tradition of portrait masks, which clearly depict individual persons and specific emotional states. The masks themselves testify in turn to a tradition of face and body painting which, no matter its representational origins, seems on or even over the verge of pure, expressive ornament. Flourishing side by side with the masks, especially among the Tlingit, there is a secondary tradition in box painting, weaving and basketry, which is closely in touch with Athapaskan geometrical abstraction.

A detailed study of northern Haida song, by John Enrico and Wendy Stuart, is now awaiting publication.

But the art is best known, as it should be, for its formline painting, relief carving and columnar sculpture, ranging from fifteen-metre housepoles to goat horn spoon handles less than a hundredth that size. In these forms, the art is distinguished by nothing so elusive as mere style, but by an actual visual language. Like a sentence, a work of Haida painting or relief carving is built primarily of known, recombinable parts subject to endless new inflections. In more fully three-dimensional work, this two-dimensional language is rent like a cloak or cracked like a shell, but fragments of the two-dimensional envelope cling to the three-dimensional form. They adhere around the orifices – eyes, nostrils, ears, mouth – of the emerging sculptural figures, and to certain flat surfaces, especially wings and tails. In well-made pieces, there is also a deeper continuity, for though the formline shell is interrupted, the rhythms and textures established in that abstract, two-dimensional language are visibly echoed and accompanied by the more realistic modeling of the three-dimensional form.

There are perhaps as few as a dozen basic recombinable elements in the language of Haida painting, but they are as supple in use as the radicals of Chinese writing. All of them could pass for stylized versions of sensory and respiratory organs – eyes, ears, gills, spines and so on. It has been customary in recent years to speak of them by more analytical names, as ovoids, U-forms, S-forms, L-forms, and these terms pay well-deserved respect to the calligraphic nature of two-dimensional Haida art, though at the same time they disguise its facial intensity and animal vitality.

These elements, like syllables, can be assembled into an infinite number of sentences. But the images which, in endless variations, reappear throughout these visual statements are without exception stylized animals. The elements are bound into the shape or map of an animal figure through a continuous primary formline, accompanied as it were by the inner organs in the form of a discontinuous secondary formline, usually red, and by tertiary hairlines or other details. The ensuing representations are quite literally all eyes and ears – with a liberal assortment of tongues, teeth, nostrils, beaks and claws attached – and the syntax linking these images is animal as well. Creatures eat, bite, swallow, disgorge and share tongues with one another; images erupt from other images. Faces emerge from the palms of hands and the soles of feet, in crotches and bellies, tails, breasts and blowholes, flippers and fins, and in the mouths, eyes and ears of other faces. Eyes stare out of hips and shoulders, ankles, nostrils, tongues.

The formal and structural beauty of these objects is relentless, but they are built resolutely of images, not of impressions. It was and still is an art tradition without gossip, without interest in what everyone can

For examples of formlines, ovoids and U-forms, see the photographs on pages 32-33. The technical terminology was developed by Bill Holm and is best explained in his book Northwest Coast Indian Art: An Analysis of Form.

The degree to which Northwest Coast formline art can be understood as animated pattern rather than patterned animation has only begun to emerge through the belatedly published research of Carl Schuster. See Schuster & Carpenter, Materials for the Study of Social Symbolism in Ancient and Tribal Art, *especially vols 1:3, 1:4 and 2:3.*

see. It has a sterner, more delicate purpose: to make visible what we know to be there but *cannot* see, and to capture for long inspection and contemplation what we would otherwise only know through fleeting glimpses.

To represent this world, the art of the Northern Coast uses an almost obsessive economy of means. The representational language uses a minimal number of elements, whose meaning shifts according to context and inflection. And the basic iconography, the lexicon of animals, is also very small. Most of the creatures in this lexicon are predators or scavengers, some ubiquitous in Haida Gwaii and others only found on the mainland. Some inhabit the surrounding sea, others reside in the ocean of imagination. This traditional bestiary is linked in part to heraldic social convention, but the real roots of the images lie in a developed body of myth.

Haida formline painting does not focus, like Magdalenian cave art, on the moment of the hunt. It dwells in the moments after: the skinning, dissecting and drying in which the animal becomes increasingly abstract. The creatures most common in Haida art are the Raven, Grizzly, Beaver, Eagle, Killer Whale, Dogfish, Frog, along with some others – all perhaps alternate forms of one another – whom white culture does not recognize as real: Waasghu, the Seawolf; Tsaghanxuuwaji, the Sea Grizzly; Taangghwanlaana, the One in the Sea; and Ttsaamuus, the Snag. None of these creatures is common in the Haida larder, yet they were treated, in Haida painting, in a manner analogous to the hunter's treatment of game. They were flayed and dissected as well as honored: rendered more abstract and, at the same moment, more tangible. The animals brought back across the *xhaaidla* by the hunter become physically as well as intellectually nourishing. Those brought to the painted surface by the artist become the guardians of this edible wealth and the emblems of its transformation. Like the hunter's prey, they also become a source of sensuous pleasure in themselves. Hunters paint and painters hunt – in different realms, for different animals, but with much the same ambitions concerning the catch.

Some of the heraldic conventions of Haida life survive; many others are lost – less from indifference than from social disintegration. A large number of the old families were wholly extinct by the early years of this century. A substantial body of Haida myth also survives, damaged and frayed like old papyrus, but every bit as rich and vital, if not as widely known, as the myths of India, Greece and Rome. And "myth" in this sense means something more than just an oft-repeated story. It means a flexible but stable tradition of philosophical narrative, which functions more in symbolic motifs and images than in descriptive or impressionistic terms.

Elaborate oral literatures and mythologies are normal in hunting and gathering societies. Stories and the voice are portable and weightless. But the peoples of the Northwest Coast embodied their myths in man-made physical objects on a scale unknown in hunting cultures anywhere else in the world. The myths surround the art; and the psychological reality, or the depth and clarity of image, that the creatures attain in myth is the source of their power in the visual art. Without that mythic depth – visible in Reid's work and in the work of his greatest predecessors – the visual art becomes only an exercise in rhetoric and logic, a study in form and design.

These are the creatures, trailing a shimmering web of interlinked stories in their silent wake, who are gathered into Reid's lifeboat, *The Spirit of Haida Gwaii*. This ark contains not only refugees from a persecuted landscape but from a persecuted literature: characters in search of further authors, and of further artists as well.

III

ARCHAEOLOGICAL finds have established the antiquity of Northwest Coast formline art; its origins and the sequence of its development remain obscure. Embryonic examples of formline art some 2500 years old have been found in what is now the Tsimshian country – then perhaps inhabited by the Tlingit. There can now be little doubt that when Europeans first encountered Northwest Coast art, in the middle of the eighteenth century, it already had behind it a sequence of indigenous development and regional variation as complex as that of European painting and sculpture. The difference is that far too little early Northwest Coast work has been found for the art history of this region to be written in similar detail.

The art appears to have no stylistic relatives among inland North American cultures. The resemblances, such as they are, lie elsewhere – around the Pacific Rim, notably among the Maori, the Ainu, and the Shang and Zhou dynasty Chinese, in early fragments from the Bering Strait, and in some pieces from coastal South America as well. It is not clear what historical connections, if any, could exist among these widely differing cultures, but the stylistic resonances remain. Stylized animals cast in bronze and carved in jade 3000 years ago in China speak a highly developed and clearly distinct visual language that nevertheless seems to belong to the same family as the two-dimensional language of the Northwest Coast. And there is a carved gourd container from Huaca Prieta – a seahunting settlement flourishing on the Peruvian coast some 5000 years ago – that may represent an early stage of another related tradition. But while all of these resemblances are intriguing, none of them is complete. The exacting visual prosody and grammar of the Northern formline, and the vibrant stillness of the ovoid – that live, organic circle, like a rising loaf – belong to the Northwest Coast alone.

Polished stone sculpture in the Northwest Coast tradition reached a very high standard, but it raises more questions than it answers. It is remarkably scarce, to begin with. Some of it is formline art, while some of it is stylistically closer to Polynesian sculpture than to other known Northwest Coast traditions. And the dates of most of these pieces remain unknown.

Metal, which was far scarcer than stone in the life of the Haida, was more prominent in their thought. Until the coming of the Europeans, the peoples of the Coast had minimal supplies of iron, obtained through

aboriginal trade or from drift wreckage originating in Asia. They also had modest supplies of apparently unrefined soft metal – native copper, bought through Tlingit middlemen from the northern Athapaskans, and used more for ornament and prestige than for practical tools.

In the world of classical Haida mythology, iron has no function. Stone is thematically important in certain contexts, while copper, *xaala*, has pride of place. Young heroes, embarking on their vision quests, insist on copper bows and arrows for shooting birds. Some of the gods wear copper blankets or travel in copper canoes. Jilaquns, the Raven's wife, like other female deities in northwestern North America, has copper fingernails as well, whose scratch will lead to wealth. Copper Woman, Xaalajaat, who appears in one extraordinary story by John Sky, cows the most powerful gods on the seafloor by flashing her eyes. Like Aphrodite, she takes a human lover, who says of her, *Hau hayinghau l ghiida*, "She is this instead of that." Her actions mean what they mean, but her words mean the inverse of what they say. In another of Sky's stories, Siixha, a chief of the village of Qquuna (Skedans) during the mythtime, owns a copper drum that gives him extraordinary power. But when the Raven catches Siixha sleeping with Jilaquns, even the drum cannot save him from the Trickster's wrath. That is the only limit I know on the power of copper in Haida myth.

If the Haida lacked the technique of metallurgy, it nevertheless lay well within their imaginative grasp, and when larger quantities of trade metal at last became available, Haida artistry in this medium reached a very high standard very quickly, even with rudimentary tools. Reid likes to joke that the bronze age came to the Northwest Coast with his first bronze sculpture, in 1984. But Haida myth had been ready and waiting for it all along.

All things considered, the Haida of precontact times do not fit comfortably into the archaeological calendar of stone, bronze and iron. They built substantial towns, elaborate houses, a hierarchical society and large, sophisticated watercraft but raised no crops, produced no pottery and made slight use of polished stone. Imaginatively, they belong in part with the Shang and Zhou to the age of metal. In most respects, they belong in a separate apartment of prehistory, lignic instead of lithic. Almost alone in North America, the Northwest Coastal peoples lived in that largest of Mediterraneans, the Pacific – and in the Age of Wood.

Stone did become a popular medium with Haida artists in historical times, but chiefly for sale to foreigners. Even then, it was stone that could be worked as wood. Black argillite – a soft, smooth, sedimentary rock, made largely of carbon and compacted clay – is found in surface quarries near Skidegate. It can be sawn and carved with woodworking tools, but it was little used by the Haida until the nineteenth century. For the European market, Haida carvers made platters, boxes, pipes, miniature housepoles, model canoes and other portable, secular objects of argillite. Some of these small sculptures portray traditional Haida themes, others show European figures, and many mix the two.

The grand master of Haida carving in argillite, and the greatest of the earlier engravers in metal, was Idansuu (1839–1924), head of the Stastas family of the Eagle side, who is known in English as Charles Edenshaw. His successor in the art, though he was born to another family and has moved to other media, is Bill Reid.

Whatever the origins of formline art, its rootedness and the tensile strength of its conventions were tested to the utmost during Edenshaw's time. In the great flux of the nineteenth century, as the population shrank by some ninety per cent and the social order crumpled, Haida art survived, even though its traditional function and audience had almost ceased to exist. Only after the holocaust, when the boarding schools had separated children from their elders, the potlatch law had prohibited the ceremonials, and missionaries had almost daily access to the remaining Island residents, did the intellectual and artistic bones and teeth of Haida life seem to follow the old social order into the ground.

In those dark days, the art grew isolated enough to qualify as modern. Artists produced everything from masterpieces of mythic thought and workmanship to bland and crude souvenirs. In some of the works of Charles Edenshaw and his contemporaries, dating from that period, Haida art also discovered, as if in proof of its own nakedness and isolation, sculpture in the round.

Until the later nineteenth century, even the three-dimensional forms in Haida sculpture seem substantially contained. For their white clientele, more often interested in cigar-store Indians and ethnographic exhibits than in representations of the mythic world, several Haida artists began to carve free-standing realistic images. Edenshaw brought this three-dimensional vision into Haida myth as well. In some of his late works, the full range from formline relief to realistic sculpture in the round is encompassed in a single piece — all without a need to distort or escape from the supple envelope of classical Haida mythology.

The importance of this example has not been lost on Reid, who has carried Haida forms and their mythic substance into other new media — European boxwood, ceramic, the silkscreen print, as well as cast gold and bronze. Reid's personal isolation from traditional Haida culture is exponentially greater than Edenshaw's, yet his art remains as deeply rooted and his task fundamentally the same. He continues, like Edenshaw, to nourish himself at that source and to speak the classical visual language of Haida culture as if the ancestors were watching, even through his white contemporaries' eyes. Speaking that silent language as he does, with an eloquence perceptible long before it is understood, he has drawn many others to taste from the old sources as well.

Argillite canoe with bone inlay, 30 cm long, by an unidentified Haida artist, late 19th century (Vancouver Museum, Vancouver). In the stern is the Grizzly Bear, sharing a tongue with his naked human wife. Amidships, facing to the port side, sits the same woman, the Bear Mother, in her later role as a widow and chief after her return among the humans. Her sons, in human form and wearing tall hats, sit flanking her, facing to starboard. In the bow, where orthodox Northwest Coast iconography would have placed the hero who rescued the Bear Mother from the bears, are three figures evidently copied from a European illustration. In place of the closed and continuous circle of the old mythology, the carver has sketched an open spectrum: from the animal in the stern, through those who have crossed the xhaaidla and have lasting, productive relations with animals, to the foreigners in the bow whose only thought concerning animals is apparently to kill them. On the starboard side near the stern is a young precursor of Reid's Ancient Reluctant Conscript.

These photographs show three sides of an argillite chest by Charles Edenshaw, undated, 45 cm wide, now in the Royal British Columbia Museum, Victoria. On the front of the chest is the face of Ttsaamuus, the Snag, or Taangghwan-laana, the One in the Sea. Here he is shown with a large spawning-salmon nose, a frontal face in each eye, a profile face in each ear, a small human face in each nostril and an inverted human face in his chin. On the rear of the chest is another upholder-of-the-world, the Beaver, with a small human face in each forepaw. The four Frogs at the base of the chest recall the Seafrog, who also lives at the base of the world. Bear cubs emerge from the ends of the chest, where one would typically find some allusion to the Raven in transition between human and avian form. Here the Raven has been promoted to the lid instead (see the photo overleaf). Edenshaw has given the Raven a human face, torso and limbs, but wings and a feathered tail, and he has both human and corvine feet. Beneath him lies the opened clamshell in which he has just discovered human beings. Like countless other shamans portrayed in sculpture from the Americas and Asia, he is inhabited by another creature as well, whose face emerges from his chest. The large beak belonging to this face is partially hidden behind and beneath the infant human he holds in his arms.

To summarize: above the lid of the chest, here at the surface of the world, the Raven within the Human within the Raven holds in his arms another human whom he has just released from within the shell of the Clam. It is a habit of the Raven in the myths to enter into the bodies of infants, and this human and corvine Raven appears poised to do just that. Below the lid of the box, which is the surface of the world, young humans and bears and other creatures emerge from the eyes, ears, nostrils, shoulders and palms of Taangghwanlaana, the One in the Sea, who himself seems in the midst of transformation into or out of human form, and whose nether face is that of the Beaver. (This is a beaver joke as well as a serious statement. The Beaver in Haida sculpture very often has a nether face, with human features, under his tail.) The house of the One in the Sea, which is this box, is the cornucopia from which all things, including humans, emerge. It rests in its turn on the back of the fourfold Frog, who is the master of wealth and transformation, as well as the Raven's own wife, child and opposite. At the six extremes of the sculpture are the Raven and the Frogs, the Beaver and Taangghwanlaana, and two young bears. Simultaneous with this six-directional hierarchy there is the formal one of flat engraving, relief carving and sculpture in the round. But this is only the beginning of a reading of this work, which in turn is only one of the important precursors of the black canoe.

Photos courtesy the Royal British Columbia Museum, Victoria, BC.

IV

BILL REID is routinely described as a Native American artist, and more specifically a Haida artist. As a statement of his racial background, this is partially true but of questionable relevance. As a statement about the kind of art he makes, however, it has substantial meaning. It is first of all a way of naming the formal tradition that his work in part defines, as one might say that Poussin is a Neoclassical artist, or Manet an Impressionist. More importantly, it is a way of naming the spiritual tradition to which, little by little, he has made himself an heir. It is a way of saying that his art presumes from the outset a relationship between humans and their world quite different from that assumed in the colonial tradition.

Reid does indeed have Haida grandparents – Haida blood, as Europeans like to say. I have not been able to find that metaphor in the world Haida storytellers portray. There, a human being holds the positions that human society and the nonhuman creatures accord him by adoption. He is *that which comes to him* and *that which he fulfills*. Haida oral literature agrees with recent European science that culture is primarily extragenetic, though it is what family wealth and genetic endowment are used continually to rebuild. The concepts of reincarnation and family loyalty are strong in the old stories, but even the boundaries between species, never mind races, are permeable and mutable in the world the Haida poets describe. The valences of love, lust and jealousy, gratitude and pride, cut through those boundaries in the stories of Walter McGregor of the Qaayahllaanas as they cut through boundaries of class in the novels of D.H. Lawrence. I suspect that the gospel of racial purity and genetic predestination, like the doctrines of Christian salvation, human preeminence and Victorian morality, came to the Northwest Coast in the baggage of Europeans.

Reid was born on 12 January 1920 in Victoria, British Columbia. His parents' home at that time was a thousand kilometres up the coast – not in Haida Gwaii, but at the town of Hyder, which clings to the mainland on the British Columbia/Alaska line, at the head of a long fjord oddly misnamed the Portland Canal. His father was an immigrant to the coast, born in Michigan of German and Scots parents. His mother was born to Haida parents in the Tsimshian country near the mouth of the Skeena River, and raised in the Haida village of Skidegate until she was sent to an Anglican boarding school near Vancouver. His maternal grandmother came from the Haida village of Tanu. Her family – and as such, the family also of her children and her daughters' children – was Qqaadasghu Qiighawaai, of the Raven side.

True to the principles she had learned in residential school, Reid's mother placed no value whatsoever on Native American culture. She raised her children as white colonials, which two out of the three of them chose to remain. Reid's curiosity drove him to investigate his aboriginal heritage, but he came to Haida art and its mythological underpinnings as everyone then had to and as most of us still must, from the outside.

The early education he contrived for himself centred on literature more than on visual art. No one who knows him remembers when his speech was not rich with allusions to and quotations from the poets – especially American and British poets of the nineteenth and early twentieth centuries. If it seems an odd upbringing for a Haida artist, it may nonetheless be as near to a traditional Haida education as the colonial white world could provide. An artist raised in the old culture would have grown up learning the inner themes of his art from the oral poets and storytellers, at the same time that he learned technique, style and iconography from the carvers. But it is likely that in the old Haida world, carver and storyteller were frequently one in the same.

In the 1940s, when Reid began to visit Haida Gwaii, he met his maternal grandfather, Charles Gladstone, and his grandfather's old friend Henry Young – men who still spoke Haida, carved on a small scale in argillite, wood and metal, and who knew the stories and songs that clung to the figures they were carving.

After a century and a half of racist discrimination, political oppression and missionization, Reid's family connection to the Haida was undoubtedly helpful to his acceptance within what remained of the Haida world. But we misunderstand his accomplishment and trivialize the challenge faced by Reid and by other Haida artists if we suppose that his racial connection with the Haida made it "natural" for him to make art in the Haida way, or conversely, that "true" Haida art can be made only by someone racially pure. The visual language, like the verbal one, is spoken only by those who have learned it. In the present world, neither language is mastered without conscious choice and labor.

Reid has lived in or adjacent to the colonial white world all his life, and he has always worked or toyed with European as well as Haida artistic forms and conventions. But little by little, he has also enacted within himself a slow and reluctant process that North American culture as a whole may have to undergo if it has any future at all. He has learned a Native American tradition from the outside in until, little by little, it could displace and redirect, from the inside out, the technologically brilliant but spiritually bankrupt colonial tradition in which he was raised.

For nearly two decades, Reid worked as a radio broadcaster, winding up with the Canadian Broadcasting Corporation in Toronto and Vancouver. In 1948, about halfway through his radio career, he also began a jewelry-making course at the Ryerson Institute in Toronto. Here he was trained exclusively in European techniques and presented with European models, but at the same time, he was studying the Haida carvings in the Royal Ontario Museum. In his apprentice jewelry work, he began almost at once to experiment with Haida as well as European design. After moving to Vancouver in 1950, he continued to do metalwork in both traditions, still supporting himself by radio announcing and script-writing. At the same time, he was reading John Swanton's translations from Haida oral literature, and the anthropological studies of Swanton, Franz Boas and others who had worked the Northwest Coast.

In 1954, in Skidegate for his grandfather's funeral, he first saw carvings by Charles Edenshaw, who had died three decades earlier, at the age of eighty-five, when Reid was four. In Edenshaw's metalwork, Reid saw perhaps for the first time the fusion of personal vision, classical language and consummate technique that has been the essence of the art for him ever since. His mature style is as different from Edenshaw's as Titian's from that of his teacher Bellini. But he began in the mid-1950s to develop a technical fluency and a supple tension of line equal to Edenshaw's. And the roster of mythcreatures who eventually took up residence in his art as shamanic familiars is very close to Edenshaw's. In the old master carver who made art in a world content with souvenirs, and incarnate myth in a world that rarely asked for more than ornaments or trinkets, Reid found the ancestor he required.

In 1956–57 he joined the British Columbia Provincial Museum team salvaging mortuary and frontal poles from Sghan-gwaai and other abandoned Haida village sites. His first experience with carving on the same scale came simultaneously, when he worked on a pole with the Kwakiutl carver Mungo Martin for two weeks during 1957. (And Martin, who despite the potlatch ban had received a fairly traditional upbringing, reinforced a lesson Reid had earlier learned from Haida carver and singer Henry Young: that literature and visual art spring from the same root. Martin sang to the wood in Kwakwala as he carved.) With that slender apprenticeship to rely on, Reid embarked in 1958 on a four-year project to carve a series of full-size poles and construct two traditional Haida houses for the University of British Columbia in Vancouver. This undertaking may have begun, in the minds of its sponsors, as an exercise in making replicas, but Reid pursued it to a deeper level of authenticity. Instead of copying, he quoted, edited and reinvented classical Haida form.

Other projects – notably his role as a consultant for a major exhibition of Northwest Coast art held in Vancouver in 1967 – brought him more opportunities to study the earlier art in close detail. Soon he was in Europe, prowling museums. He spent 1968–69 chiefly in London, pursuing further study in goldsmithing, and the next three years in Montreal, where some of his finest pieces both Haida and European were made. But when he returned to Vancouver in 1973, he was diagnosed as a victim of Parkinson's disease, which has since placed heartbreaking limits on his ability to do direct carving.

Direct knifework means much in Haida art, especially to a craftsman as exacting as Reid, and it is, of course, missing from his bronzes. They are as smooth as sandpapered wood, while the old tradition preferred the surface left by knife and adze. His disease has deprived him of that sensuous involvement with surface, and that tactile form of personal signature. Yet the intensity of his conception and design work has steadily increased, and with it the power of his modeling.

A quick catalogue of his most significant pieces in the Haida tradition would include, in addition to *The Spirit of Haida Gwaii*, at least the following:

Illustrations of all these pieces can be found in Doris Shadbolt's book Bill Reid (*1986*).

- The suite of five poles and two houses carved in 1958–62 for the University of British Columbia, Vancouver;

- The small boxwood carving of *The Raven Discovering Mankind in the Clam Shell* (1970) and the large yellowcedar version of the same theme, *The Raven and the First Men* (1983), both now in the University of British Columbia's Museum of Anthropology, Vancouver;

- The frontal pole for the Haida Council House in Skidegate (1978);

- The bronze *Killer Whale* at the Vancouver Aquarium (1984) and its tiny, now damaged, boxwood original (1983);

- The series of pencil drawings for *The Raven Steals the Light*, culminating in the drawing of the Dogfish Woman (1983, published in book form 1984);

- The black bronze frieze entitled *Mythic Messengers* (1985), at the Teleglobe Canada building in Burnaby, BC, with a duplicate at the Museum of Civilization, Ottawa;

- The redcedar carving *Phyllidula, the Shape of Frogs to Come* (1985), Vancouver Art Gallery;

- The suite of painted dugout canoes, built in 1983–86 and culminating in the *Luu Tas* ("Wave Eater"), now in use in Haida Gwaii;

- A number of small pieces in gold and silver beginning about 1964 and dating over a period of more than twenty years.

Phyllidula, the Shape of Frogs to Come
(1985), yellowcedar, 126 cm long,
Vancouver Art Gallery.

Overleaf: *The Raven Discovering Mankind
in the Clam Shell* (1970), boxwood, 7 cm
high, in Reid's hands, and the larger
version, *The Raven and the First Men*
(1983), yellowcedar, 210 cm high,
University of British Columbia Museum of
Anthropology.

Three of the items on this list – comprising half a dozen poles and three canoes – are living reincarnations of archaic traditional forms, and several are now in traditional use, not in museums. Three other items – *The Killer Whale* in bronze, together with the small and large versions of *The Raven and the First Men* and *Phyllidula*, which are all in wood – are traditional images from the Haida bestiary, developed along the line begun by Edenshaw, as free-standing sculptures in the round. Their Haida antecedents include a type of traditional sculpture called the *manda* (a free-standing coffin-rest) as well as the smaller nineteenth-century carvings in wood and argillite. But in the suppleness and intensity of his forms, Reid has moved far beyond these models. He has reached much farther than Edenshaw into the well-lit, sensuous world of three-dimensional space, still without losing touch or breaking faith with the world of Haida myth and its iconographic tradition.

Mythic Messengers, in black bronze, is yet another variation on nineteenth-century argillite carving. It is an argillite panel pipe, enlarged to monumental size, but informed with a fluidity, lyricism and design sense that the souvenir pipes of the last century rarely or never attained. Made on commission for a harsh commercial environment, it is a sonata emerging suddenly from a lineage of études and bagatelles: a tiny form made open enough and potent enough to thrive on a monumental scale.

Reid's work in precious metal is directly descended from nineteenth-century Haida metalwork – Edenshaw's in particular – but its ultimate antecedents lie deeper than that. His important pieces in this medium are for the most part of three kinds: miniature chests, miniature masks in the form of pendants or brooches, and wide metal bracelets. The connection of these masks and containers with traditional Northwest Coast forms is obvious enough, and the bracelets have an equal link with the tradition. They are, in effect, small dancing blankets, like the one that covers the shoulders of the Chief in *The Spirit of Haida Gwaii*. They are the hides of the mythcreatures, flayed alive and symmetrically displayed: living skins that engulf and transform the wearer. As bracelets, they do so only in token form, like a shaman's charm, by encircling the wrist. But as gold or silver, they are honorary and superlative forms of copper – that substance of which, in the myths, only the blankets of the sons and daughters of the gods are made.

The remaining item on my minimum list of important pieces is a series of pencil drawings. These again have Haida precursors. Pencil drawings by Edenshaw, John Cross, Tom Price and other nineteenth-century carvers appear in several museum collections. But Reid's drawings are drastically different in character, much woodier than their predecessors. They are two-dimensional graphite sculptures, whittled up instead of down. At the other extreme from the fluent line drawing of the Magdalenian draftsmen, Matisse or Picasso, they were built up as painstakingly as an adzed surface in wood or pitted repoussé in metal.

I think those late works in pencil are also the first in which Reid bridged the iconographic gap between humans and the other animals. Human beings had appeared in his work from time to time over the years, but never with the same convincing presence as the spirit creatures. In those drawings – apart from the crowd of tiny, rather lice-like men emerging from the clamshell – Reid's humans have joined the immortal, indigenous crew. They are sculpted of imaginary wood with nothing more than a graphite pencil, yet they have worked their way so deeply into the art it has brought them alive. They are also, as it happens, the immediate precursors of Reid's most intense political writings on the subject of aboriginal land rights and the human place in the world of Haida Gwaii.

Reid is a visual artist who began by studying literature and who made his living by the spoken word for close to twenty years. His writing, which has the broad and keen oratorical edge of the poetry he most admires, has continued from the 1950s to the present day.

His decision to focus primarily on visual art is, I think, a paradoxical consequence of his increasing understanding of and allegiance to a culture in which that very specialization was unlikely to occur. While "Indian legends" are eagerly received, no practical possibilities for making a living through an authentic Haida literary voice have yet emerged. But the eye of the white culture is much wider than its inner ear. In the visual arts, Reid found it possible to speak quite seriously and intently from one culture and be listened to, even if not understood, in another.

When his pilgrimage back to Haida mythology began, Reid faced problems and limitations scarcely different from those that confront his own audience now. The traders that preyed and encroached on Haida Gwaii had a purpose in mind for the old works of visual art. These could be sold for exhibit in private collections and public museums in Europe and the United States. But the stories, dances and songs that attached to the carvings had far less commercial potential in a world whose cultural curiosity stopped at collecting souvenirs. The visual language also looks (deceptively) much easier to master than the spoken. Despite his verbal skills and instincts, Reid's communion with Haida mythology, like almost everyone's in this century, has therefore come chiefly through visual means.

But in recent years, even some of the creatures of Haida mythology who have little or no presence in the old visual art have begun to emerge in his work. And there is no doubt of the personal intensity and depth that some of the mythcreatures have for him. The Raven, the Bear

These drawings are reproduced in Reid & Bringhurst, The Raven Steals the Light.

Reid's major publications are listed at the end of this volume, but much of his best writing is still uncollected. His earliest known piece of writing is a eulogy for his grandfather, broadcast on CBC radio in 1954. Like much of his work, it has been published in oral but not in written form.

43

Mother, the Frog, the Dogfish Woman and the Ttsaamuus or Snag have become Reid's powerful familiars. And they have attained through him a living presence in the outer world that they achieve only in the work of the finest Haida poets and sculptors. No one, I think, was more surprised than Reid himself when these creatures found their way into his work, for they had hardly been seen or heard from since the deaths of Charles Edenshaw and the two great Haida poets who were his contemporaries: Walter McGregor and John Sky.

These mythcreatures were waiting in Reid's mind in 1985, when Arthur Erickson asked him to make a sculpture for the entry court of the new Canadian chancery in Washington, DC, which Erickson had designed. Erickson's first proposal, a pair of Haida welcome figures, posed a problem of authenticity. Welcome figures are found on the southern coast, not in Haida Gwaii. But some of the nineteenth-century argillite canoes Reid had seen in museum collections were moving through his mind, along with the series of redcedar dugouts, culminating in the *Luu Tas*, which had occupied him over the previous three years. He proposed to Erickson that the court contain, instead of welcome figures, travellers: several figures in a large canoe.

V

BECAUSE Reid's conception of the sculpture stemmed from argillite carving, he saw it from the outset in black. Indeed, his original intention was to carve it in black granite. But after discussing the limitations of the medium with his assistant and technical advisor George Rammell, Reid abandoned the idea of granite in favor of something more supple: black patinated bronze.

He began work on a small clay sketch in the spring of 1986. Toward the end of that year, Rammell cast a plaster model at the same size (about a metre long) from the unfinished clay, but a political confrontation interrupted the work at this stage. Protests against continued clearcut logging in southern Haida Gwaii had become intense, while land claims negotiations and plans for a national park in the area were stalled by disputes between the federal and provincial governments. During much of 1987, Reid pointedly refused to work on a sculpture destined for a Canadian government building.

The Haida blockade against logging on Lyell Island lasted nearly two years, and Reid himself was directly involved in the dispute only for the last few months. But the political issue that underlay it reaches a long distance backward and forward in time and is deeply embedded in the sculpture.

In what we can know now of earlier Haida thought – through what survives of earlier Haida art and oral literature – the world is "owned" by the beings, human and nonhuman, who *are* the world. This view is, of course, not shared by all Haida of the present day, and it may never have been shared by all Haida at any time in the past. But in the world of Haida myth, the world is owned by trees, bears and fish as well as human beings, and in particular it is owned by killer whales, who are the animating spirits of the streams, mountains, cliffs, islands, reefs and the oceans themselves. The Haida of earlier days, like those of the present, were intensely territorial, but Haida myth, like European science, exposes the frailty of human claims to power. The mythtellers remind us that human beings are neither the most essential nor the most responsible of creatures sharing the earth. They portray a world in which the jurisdiction of surface people, *xhaaidla xhaaidaghai*, therefore does not go very deep.

In the colonial view, of course, the world is owned by humans alone, though claims are laid on behalf of individuals, corporations and the state, which in Canada still calls itself the crown. In Canadian law, moreover, oceans and air are federally controlled, while land and forests are owned in the first instance by the provinces. The dispute in southern Haida Gwaii soon crystallized, therefore, into a contest between the provincial and federal governments. The former sided with its clients, the logging corporations, while the latter sided with the tourist industry and thus, momentarily and to a limited degree, with environmental interests. Public sentiment against continued logging was achieved through persistent and well-publicized Haida statements and demonstrations, but the Haida position remained officially unacknowledged, and the Haida claim to continued sovereignty in the Islands was pointedly ignored. The dispute was resolved, if that is the word, by the promise of a large payment of money from the federal to the provincial government, for timber, surface and subsurface rights in Haida Gwaii — a territory in which, from the Haida point of view, neither government had more rights than a passing storm.

Ludicrous though it seemed to many Haida and white observers, this compromise achieved the most immediate of several desired results. Once the federal-provincial agreement was negotiated, what is known to the Haida as *Gwaii Haanas*, the Islands of Awe, became in the drier language of the federal government the South Moresby National Park Reserve — and logging in southern Haida Gwaii was halted at last.

Reid then resumed his work on the sculpture. In early 1988, George Rammell and the crew constructed a full-size prototype in clay over a steel armature. Some of the figures were scaled up with a profile gauge and templates from the plaster model; others, which were less resolved in the model, were roughed in on the basis of Reid's sketches and verbal directions. Reid then worked at the large clay prototype throughout the spring, refining and balancing the forms. By early summer, a complete plaster mold had been built over the large clay prototype. The mold was equipped with a series of doors and lids, giving access to the clay within. Through these aperatures, Rammell and the crew then excavated the clay and its steel armature from the mold, and *The Spirit of Haida Gwaii* became pure negative space.

In the fall of 1988, working within the hollow mold, Rammell designed and built a new and more complex armature: modules of welded angle-iron bolted together with stainless steel. Between the armature and the mold, a full-size plaster positive was then cast. Like the armature that supported it, this plaster pattern was built in sections that could be removed one by one to the shop floor for revision as required. Reid then recarved the figures repeatedly in this medium. Some sections of the pattern were repeatedly destroyed, their armatures rewelded, and the figures carved anew.

46

In late 1989, the completed plaster pattern, engineered by Rammell into a three-dimensional jigsaw puzzle of more than a hundred pieces, was completely dismantled in Reid's Vancouver studio. Each component was coated with white shellac to stabilize the plaster, and the fully disassembled pattern was crated and shipped to the Tallix Foundry in Beacon, New York. After Rammell and several assistants reassembled the plaster pattern on the foundry floor, it was again disassembled and partly resectioned for casting.

The foundry processes — casting and gating in wax, dipping the wax to produce sectional ceramic molds, casting and chasing each section in bronze, and welding the hundred-odd pieces of cast bronze into one — occupied all of 1990. In the meantime, Reid remained unsatisfied with the plaster pattern for the speaker's staff held by the central figure in the canoe. He commissioned a young Haida carver, Don Yeomans, to carve the staff anew in yellowcedar, and approved this pattern for casting late in 1990. The plaster pattern for the small killer whale that surmounts the staff was discarded as well and a new version modeled directly in wax by George Rammell in January 1991, five years after Reid had made his early sketches.

The final welding, chasing and patinating — with blowtorch, brush and a solution of copper nitrate — were completed the following month. The surface was then treated against exposure with commercial black shoe polish: a substance many Haida carvers have used in recent years to finish argillite sculpture.

In one of the poems of Reid's predecessor, John Sky of Tanu, a deputation of surface people arrives by canoe in front of the house of one of the earth-shaking beings with protruding eyes who live on the floor of the sea. Once they position themselves offshore, on the ocean at the bottom of the ocean, and tie themselves into their seats, they and their canoe are lifted by a bolt of feathered lightning and dropped through the smokehole into the house.

On the day of installation, 19 November 1991, the black canoe with all its passengers aboard was hoisted by a crane and lowered through the open smokehole of Arthur Erickson's building, settling in the Canadian chancery's shallow courtyard pool. On the bow of the boat, the Bear sits facing backwards, cradling one of his halfbreed sons. The Raven is steering him straight for the Capitol dome.

VI

NOT COUNTING stowaways, there are thirteen passengers in the canoe. At first sight, four of them are humans and three of them are bears, two are rodents, two are birds, one is a wolf and one an amphibian. On closer acquaintance, all of them have, in their wardrobe of inner identities, human forms. And of those who appear uncompromisingly human, one is part fish, one is married to a bear and has borne him two cubs, one is wearing the hide of a finned and Argus-eyed quadruped, and the last is dressed in the bark of a tree.

1 XUUYA / THE RAVEN

At the heart of the Haida intellectual world, and of Reid's world also, is the Raven: in his usual incarnation, a songless yet sonorous, polyglot bird. But he is more protean than that. He is bluegreen, white, or black, as occasion may require; he is male or female, human or avian, or if need be, mineral, vegetable or fish. He is beautiful, shameless, lazy, vain, yet incessantly active, curious, hungry, salacious, quick to disinterest, yet for preference monogamous. He is so widely travelled in time and space that he is his own uncle and nephew. His agenda, if he has one, is secret even from himself. But he was in the white time before anything was and will be in the black timelessness after.

He has many names in Haida, but when his intrusions into the order of things are seen, it is sufficient to say, *Hau iijins hau iijaaghan*: "It's the one it usually is." As lovely as the night sky, as immortal as the cockroach, he finds his way to everything worth having, but his greed is our gain, for when he has stolen it for himself, he will lose it or tire of it soon, or in a fit of generosity, he will deliberately give it away. One way or another, it will be shared. This is how sunlight, moonlight, dirt, trees, fish, fresh water, good weather and sexual pleasure came to be spread throughout the world. Ex nihilo, from scratch, he creates nothing. To judge from appearances, which is dangerous, he is often along for nothing more than the ride. But no one else could steer this canoe — and he is steering.

Raven stories, like Coyote stories, are legion, but Haida poets of the nineteenth century divided them into a "sacred" and a "profane" series, known as the Old Man's and the Young Man's stories. Substantial portions of the Haida Raven epic were recorded a century ago in Victoria by Charles Edenshaw of the Stastas, in Skidegate by John Sky of the Qquuna Qiighawaai and Walter McGregor of the Qaayahllaanas, and at Masset by Walter of the Ghau Sttlanlnagaai, Isaac of the Hlyaalang Qiighawaai, and Peter of the Kyanusili. Translations of these were published by John Swanton. Franz Boas's Tsimshian Mythology includes comparative summaries of Raven stories from throughout the Northwest Coast. Reid's versions of some of the stories are told in Reid & Bringhurst, The Raven Steals the Light.

It is a circumpolar story, known in various guises among Algonkian, Athapaskan and Siberian peoples, and once central in the ritual life of the Ainu of Japan. The Greeks twisted it slightly, to give Zeus more room, and told it as the story of Kallisto, the Bear woman, daughter of the Wolf chief, Lykaon. The story is enshrined in that form even now in the northern constellations Ursa Minor and Ursa Major, the Cub and the Great Bear – though few astronomers (or astrologers, for that matter) may now be able to give a credible version.

Some people tell it of black bears, who live in the Islands, and some of brown bears, grizzlies, who keep to the mainland. The story takes many forms, and perhaps it has happened many times on the Northwest Coast, and perhaps it will until every watershed has been cleared, measured and fenced into parking lots or gardens. But once, a woman made loud, derogatory statements about grizzlies, after she'd slipped in a pile of rich, fruity bear dung. Later that day, a well-dressed, well-mannered young man emerged from the berry patch to help her with her load. He guided her to a town behind the mountain which she had never heard of or seen. It was peopled by grizzlies, who removed their outer skins as they entered their houses. Within, they looked and spoke like human beings.

Grizzlies, like all wild creatures, are sensitive to what is said about them, and little escapes their ears. Stung by the woman's insults, the bears were keenly interested in her own droppings. They wanted to know if she could do better. By carefully burying her turds, and leaving broken bits of her copper jewelry in their place on top of the ground, she convinced her captors that she was fully entitled to criticize.

Despite the success of this ruse, or because of it, a strong bond developed between the woman and the bears. She married the grizzly town chief's son and bore him two male children.

The Bear Mother's brothers were searching for her all this while. They discovered her, many storytellers say, and when they did so, another challenge faced them. In rescuing their sister and avenging her abduction, the brothers were required to kill the bear. Yet these same brothers, as the cubs' maternal uncles, were charged with overseeing their education, raising the cubs as their own heirs. Reid has caught the figures – Bear Mother, Bear Father and two cubs – before the final act of this complex tragedy befalls.

Farther south along the coast, it was known that the Bear Mother's children grew up to be the Transformers: two or four brothers whose function in life was much like the Raven's. Transformers and Trickster alike are out to adjust the balance of the world, to keep the degree of equilibrium from becoming too great or too little. Reid has given them some equilibrium to adjust among themselves as well, and likes to call the cubs Good Bear and Bad Bear, citing as his authority another mythteller by the name of A.A. Milne.

There is a certain disaffection between the Raven and the Grizzly, which may explain their positions, facing each other from opposite ends of the canoe. In the early days of the world, when the Raven took the Grizzly out fishing for halibut, he convinced him that fresh testicles were the best of all possible bait. The trusting Grizzly wounded himself mortally trying to follow the Raven's advice, and grizzlies have been reluctant to ride in the same boat with ravens ever since. Their presence here together, even if they are as far apart as they can get, speaks of the urgency of their errand.

3 GHUUT / THE EAGLE

In the Haida social order, Eagle and Raven are coequal. They stand for the Two Halves. They are both powerful creatures in the mythology as well, but Eagle stories are few, while the Raven leaves an endless chain of narrative marking his path.

There is a poignant Haida story about a man who crosses the *xhaaidla* to become an eagle, through marriage and adoption. But like many Haida stories reaching beyond the human world, it is rooted in the matrix of human weakness and desire. Walter of the Qaayahllaanas begins his recorded version with these words:

Nang laana augha hau naadalang jaaghang inaghiihldaxidang wansuuga.
La ghal qaa'idisi kkyahl waghei gausghwaananggangasi.
Ttsanughaalanga la daghaan l suuwus, la daudaasi,
gyan wagheixhan gausghwaananggangasi.
Qquuji at kkyaalu la daghaghaawun l suuwus,
gii la axhadaaghadasi, wagheixhan gausghwaananggangasi.
Han la istaghandixhan tlaahlinggisghwaansingghu hailaawang wansuuga.
Gyan l daughan-gha ghan unsatdaahlsi.

The village chief was usually a man. His title was nonetheless laana augha, *Town Mother.*

One who was Town Mother permitted his nephews to lie with his wife,
    they say.
He always escorted them out, and they didn't return.
He said that he owned a dry tree, and he sent them to fetch it,
and then they didn't return.
He owned treebark, a cormorant too, he said.
He sent them for those, and again they didn't return.
He continued like this until nine had vanished, they say.
And then their younger brother came to know.

The headman's nephews are his heirs. It is not abnormal in Haida myth that the senior nephew should assume the wife along with the rest of his uncle's privileges and obligations, nor that the wife should acquire the nephew as a rejuvenated husband. Nor is it abnormal that this transition should begin while the uncle is still alive. The apparent danger in this scene is the saturnine uncle's jealous wish to preempt his heirs. By refusing to be succeeded, he refuses to be reborn – though to read it another way, he may simply be exercising his duty to test his nephews, to see which is worthy to serve as his spiritual grandson.

The tenth and youngest nephew, whose shamanic or spiritual powers exceed his uncle's, survives the traps that have killed his brothers. Unable to murder his youngest nephew, the old shaman fastens him into a box and sets him adrift. In time, the chest washes up on an island inhabited by eagles, who adopt their human castaway rather than enslave him. Like the grizzlies, the eagles are seen to shift in and out of human form, and the young man marries the daughter of the eagles' Town Mother or village chief. He has other adventures, which reveal that the old grandmother, with her dulled claws, stiff wings and tattered feathers, is nonetheless the most powerful of the eagles. Rescued from death or reborn through her agency, the young nephew returns in eagle form to the human world, where he grasps his uncle in his talons and casts him into the sea. *L qaagha ising siis yagu sghaanaghwaghyalang wansuuga. Hau tlan l gheida*, Walter says: "His uncle became a god in mid-ocean, they say. Here it ends."

There is an overt reference to this story in at least one of Reid's works, *Mythic Messengers*, in which a human form emerges from the Eagle's beak. Here in the black canoe, the allusions are hidden. Is this the human in Eagle form, or the Eagle in Eagle form? If the Raven steering this boat is male, which he somehow seems to be, is this not likely to be the female Eagle? The Eagle who took a human husband, grasping the hand of the Grizzly who married a human wife? She or he is in any case the emblem of the Other Side. Gods, humans, mountains and everything living, which is everything there is, are all necessarily divided in Haida cosmology into two halves, Eagle and Raven, precisely so they can come together again.

4 GHUUTS / THE WOLF

So far as I know, Reid has yet to make any use of the Haida story of the wolf cub adopted by a human father. It is another of those tales in which a human is privileged to visit an animal town, though in this case the visit is brief. Adoption rather than marriage creates the human-animal bond, and the adoption takes place on this side of the line. Tom Stevens of the Naikun Qiighawaai told this story and some others in Skidegate in 1901, while John Swanton was there to write them down, and the story may be waiting somewhere now at the back of Reid's mind. Wolf stories are scarce in Haida Gwaii, and real wolves, like grizzlies, nonexistent. Even in the visual art of the Haida, the Wolf is not a common figure. But it has a special importance to Reid since it is a principal crest of his family, the Qqaadasghu Qiighawaai. From tooth to tail, this wolf is singularly wolflike. Only the forepaws, with which he grasps his paddle, reveal that he too owns a human form.

5 HLKKYAAN QQUSTTAAN / THE FROG

The frogs of Haida Gwaii aren't frogs; they are northern toads, which early white visitors misidentified. Most English-speaking Haida still prefer to call them frogs, and this translation of the Haida name, *hlkkyaan qqusttaan*, is now standard. A more literal translation would be "bush crab." *Hlkkyaan* means forest or backwoods; *qqusttaan* (from *qqu*, to bite) is a Dungeness crab.

Much of Haida art and culture comes from the sea, but the myths are peopled also by a crucial group of female figures who live in the headwaters of streams. These are the Qaasghajiina, the Creek Women. Perhaps the seniormost of them is Jilaquns, the Raven's wife and the grandmother of the Eagle side of the Haida. Her first familiar, whom she sometimes calls her child, is the Frog. Jilaquns's creek, near the old village site of Hlqinnuhl, or Cumshewa, on the east coast of southern Haida Gwaii, is a polluted little drainage through the slash of an old logging operation now. The mythtellers of the future may mention clearcut logging by name. Those of the past used other images to make their point, that human insults to the Creek Women are sooner or later avenged.

In nature, northern toads, or Haida frogs, have long, quick tongues hinged at the front of the mouth, very few bones and no teeth, although they are carnivores. And no creature native to the Islands passes so visibly through such amazing transformations. In the art, the Frog is often found sharing his tongue with another creature, or emerging, through another creature's mouth, from the wet, invisible inner world. The Frog, like insects and fish, but unlike mammals and birds in classical Haida sculpture, is frequently given perfectly circular, lidless eyes. Reid has pulled the traditional form to its limit here (as in his earlier Frog *Phyllidula*) by making the eyes hemispherical.

Throughout northwestern North America, the Frog is a talisman of wealth as well as a migrant between realms. In Haida cosmology, as his name implies, the Frog's original place is in the sea. And as Haida elder

Margaret Blackman, During My Time: Florence Edenshaw Davidson, a Haida Woman, p. 70.

Florence Davidson has explained, "If you come across anything from the sea in the woods, it's a lucky sign. You eat it for luck and you keep the shells in a bentwood box. After that it's easy to get anything; you become richer and richer."

Moving in and out of the water, in and out of the mouth, the Frog knows more than other creatures about the elusiveness of things, as well as about the powers of sexuality and transformation. He breathes in air as well as water, trades a tail for legs in middle life, and swallows his own skin when he molts. How can these un-Newtonian miracles be? Yet we confront them every day, in birth and death and making love, and in acts as simple as eating and speaking.

6 QAGANJAAT / THE MOUSE WOMAN

Tucked like a stowaway under the body of the Raven, the Mouse Woman is the smallest figure in the canoe. She is also arguably the oldest, for though the Raven has always existed, he is her grandson.

The Mouse Woman is known all over the Northwest Coast, as *Qaganjaat* in Haida, *Ksemwuttsiin* in Tsimshian, *Ha'la'malagha* in Kwakwala, *Kagákk'ushànák'w* in Tlingit. Her sisters farther afield take other identities, like the Spider Grandmother, *Kookyangwwuuti*, of the Hopi. She is the advisor of those who have crossed, or are about to cross, the *xhaaidla*, the surface of the world. It was she, for instance, who taught the Bear Mother how to protect herself with copper in the village of the bears.

Qaganjaat rarely appears in Haida visual art — only here and there on the handle of a goat horn spoon — but this is not her first canoe trip. John Sky tells of her guiding a Haida canoe to the bottom of the sea.

The son of Nangdldastlas, the submarine deity of Hecate Strait, once came to court a Haida girl, whose parents had refused all human suitors. When the young god's offer of marriage, like everyone else's, was refused, Sky says, the god kidnapped the girl. But by way of a bridal gift, he left his father's hat, which he had borrowed without permission. And it was no ordinary hat. Surf crashed on its brim. Sandpipers and turnstones flew out from it and returned. The one who wore it could raise a tidal wave by wrinkling his brow.

To rescue a human taken in marriage by a god, potent help was required. The kidnapped girl's two brothers therefore went out to get superhuman wives. One of them chose (or was chosen by) the most powerful wife he could find, Xaalajaat, Copper Woman, and the other married the wisest, Qaganjaat, the Mouse Woman. Both went along, by canoe, on the rescue mission to the seafloor, where they returned Nangdldastlas's hat and retrieved the girl.

All three mixed marriages seem to end at this moment, but one of them has issue. Nangdldastlas himself was reborn as his own grandson to the rescued girl, in her parents' house in Haida Gwaii. She and her family, following his strict instructions, placed the baby in a cradle painted with cumulus clouds, paddled it out to the middle of Hecate Strait and dropped it over the side. The cradle turned round and round to the right as it sank, and the rejuvenated god provided fish and good fishing weather in return for the gift of rebirth through the body of a woman.

One of the things that distinguish the stories of Sky and McGregor is their interest in the complex symbiosis between mythcreatures and humans. Edenshaw and Reid as well show this penetrating interest in the highly charged relations between the inhabitants of the seen and unseen worlds. Reid likes to speak of Qaganjaat as a *literary device*, but her presence here, in the organic shelter formed by the Raven's tail, proves her to be, as in Sky's and McGregor's stories, something more.

7 QQAAXHADAJAAT / THE DOGFISH WOMAN

The dogfish is a small shark common in the inshore waters of the Northwest Coast and a major crest figure in Haida art. But the Dogfish Woman is more enigmatic. Her story is one of many strands in the web of Haida mythology now broken, though not perhaps entirely beyond repair. We have, at least, some filaments of information.

The anthropologist Franz Boas heard a summary of her story more than a century ago, possibly from Charles Edenshaw. In 1900, Edenshaw mentioned her again, in a cryptic sentence, to John Swanton. Edenshaw drew and carved her image repeatedly, and Reid has been driven to do the same. He began in the 1950s making copies of some of Edenshaw's Dogfish Women, and his later studies of this figure have attained a rare intensity. Unfathomable strangeness coupled with deep recognition and resemblance, such as men confront in women and women in men, is present in this shark who is a woman. Empathy and incomprehension, gentleness and fury, beauty and ugliness, self and other, coexist in her. In her lost story, somehow the attraction between sexes and the barrier between species coincide.

As Boas heard it, a married woman used to poke fun at dogfish – perhaps for having two penises (*qqaaxhii* in Haida), as all sharks do. A dogfish caught the woman up one day and took her to visit his people. In time, she grew fins and gills, though her face was still recognizably human. Her human husband discovered her years later, but could not persuade her to return – or did not try.

So we know at least that among the stories of Qqaaxhadajaat was another of those tales of a human being crossing the *xhaaidla* and being adopted on the other side. She is a woman who has realized, as any human might, her dual citizenship in the human and nonhuman realms. We also know, from the intensity of the images, that there is more to the myth than this précis reveals. The other surviving clue is Edenshaw's statement to Swanton, that the Dogfish Woman is the sister of Nangdldastlas, the deity of Hecate Strait who was reborn to his own daughter-in-law.

Here in the black canoe, the Dogfish Woman is also a counterimage to the Bear Mother, though both are paddling on the same side and in the same direction. In Haida art, the Woman who Married the Bear is constantly shown with her ursine husband and children, while the Dogfish Woman always appears alone, as a kind of wandering divorcée, lost between realms. I was in the studio one day when Reid was at work on the plaster pattern. Both women's heads had been hauled off their shoulders and propped on stands for fine tuning. The Bear Mother looked alarmingly noble. "The Statue of Liberty?" someone asked. "Yes," Reid said, moving on to the Dogfish Woman's head. "And the Statue of Tyranny."

Superficially at least, she is more human here than in many other versions. She has the dogfish's gills on her cheeks, and the dogfish's vertical pupils, but no fins. And she wears a dogfish crown, which Reid has forged into a link between Haida and French neoclassicism.

Her hooked nose is a traditional sign of metamorphosis in Haida art. She is eating and breathing herself, reminding us that digestion and respiration, present in all of us, are two of the deepest mysteries of transformation. (The hook is often described as a hawk's nose, and creatures equipped with it often misidentified as hawks. Its more probable origin is the hooked nose of the spawning male salmon.) This Dogfish Woman also looks younger than Reid has usually depicted her. Perhaps she is still riding the tail of puberty – another form of transformation no less mysterious and astonishing than the others.

8 TTSAANG / THE BEAVER

As a crest, the Beaver has been claimed by most Haida families of the Eagle side, but it is another of those crests that may have come to the Islands through immigration, intermarriage, adoption or purchase from the mainland. There were no actual beaver in Haida Gwaii until their limited introduction in 1950.

The Beaver is nevertheless a charmingly complex creature in Haida mythology. He was one of the Raven's early adoptive uncles, from each of whom the Raven stole what he could before continuing on his way.

From the Beaver, the Raven stole the house itself and all its surroundings – the lake, the stream, the trout and salmon that swam in it, the berry bushes growing close around and, most importantly, the fish trap. The Raven presented all these gifts to Jilaquns, the Lady of the Frogs, his bride, when he brought her to the Islands. All, that is, except the fish trap, which he kept hidden under his wing.

But the Beaver has prodigious, renewable wealth in the world of Northwest Coast mythology, just as the Raven has prodigious, renewable life and a kind of immortal, feckless poverty (and the Grizzly, despite the Raven, prodigious virility). The Raven can be killed, but he is promptly reborn. The Beaver can be embezzled, but his wealth remains. And the Beaver – an aquatic, housebuilding, alien creature – was absorbed into Haida mythology as an alternate form of a more enigmatic being, the Ttsaamuus or Snag. His alternate or subsidiary forms are the Seawolf and the Seabear, or Sea Grizzly. The stories of all these creatures intersect, with the Raven's story and others, on the ocean floor, at the base of the original stone housepole.

The Snag, who lives on the floor of the sea, is the source of all wealth. His image or that of his grandfather or uncle, Taangghwanlaana, the One in the Sea, is painted and carved on the sides of countless chests and boxes made on the Northwest Coast, as an emblem of the wealth they were intended to contain. At the base of his housepole sits the Sea Frog, and the crown of the pole is awash like a waterlogged tree.

But the Snag and his usual incarnations – Seawolf and Sea Grizzly – are all crests belonging to the Raven side; the Beaver is a crest of the Eagle side. So the Beaver often appears, in place of the Snag, at the base of Eagle family memorial poles, wearing the Snag's tall hat with many rings. And the hat itself, another symbol of wealth, is an alternate metaphor for the submarine housepole which is the axis of the world.

9 THE ANCIENT RELUCTANT CONSCRIPT

The paddler in the stern position on the starboard side is not the first self-portrait in Haida art, but he is one of few, and no creature in the canoe went through more revisions. It was Reid who christened him, while the sculpture was still in its infancy, after an early Carl Sandburg poem, "Old Timers":

> I am an ancient reluctant conscript.
>
> On the soup wagons of Xerxes I was a cleaner of pans.
>
> On the march of Miltiades' phalanx I had a haft and head;
> I had a bristling gleaming spear-handle.

Red-headed Caesar picked me for a teamster.
He said, "Go to work, you Tuscan bastard,
Rome calls for a man who can drive horses."

. . .

Lincoln said, "Get into the game; your nation takes you."
And I drove a wagon and team and I had my arm shot off
At Spotsylvania Court House.

I am an ancient reluctant conscript.

See "The Spirit of Haida Gwaii," Natural History, in press for 1991 or 1992.

He is well but unostentatiously dressed, in his cedarbark cape and plain-woven spruce root hat. He matches closely with John Sky's description of a supernaturally gifted slave who makes the voyage with Qaganjaat and others to the bottom of the sea. But Reid has described him elsewhere as, above all, a survivor – a name he also used to give to his old collaborator and friend the anthropologist Wilson Duff. These are all parts of the truth. Another part, surely, is that every creature in the canoe is part of the fluid crystal of Haida mythology, and yet possesses an identity that is his or hers alone, and yet again is a facet, a partial portrait, of Bill Reid.

10 KILSTLAAI / THE CHIEF

"I don't know who he is, but he had her once and lost her," Reid said later in an interview with filmmaker Alan Clapp.

"Who is he? That's the big question," Reid said to me in the studio one day when the sculpture was still in progress. I don't believe he was kidding. The question seems to me central to the sculpture, and I think this question is hard enough to keep asking itself for some time. *Who Is He* is also not a bad name for a chief. It might have appealed to many of the old Haida whom Reid admires. Theirs was a society in which social rank meant a great deal, yet their literature is full of stories in which orphans and castaways rise to the top.

Kilstlaai, meaning the spokesman, the exemplar, the director, is at the same time an allusion to the Raven, whose favorite name in human form is *Nangkilstlas*, One Who Gives Orders. But this is a name the Raven's uncles and grandfathers bore even before the world was made. As a child, the Raven's name was *Nangkilstlas Hlingaai*, Nangkilstlas-to-be.

The Chief is dressed in his regalia, he is standing amidships in the canoe, and he is holding in his right hand a speaker's staff. He is ready, it seems, for the canoe to come to shore, ready to start dancing as he disembarks, and he expects to find someone to speak to. In the myths, all chiefs of any importance are shamans as well. And no human of ordinary attainments would be standing in the midst of such a menagerie.

His steersman is the Raven, and his familiars include all the primary icons of Haida mythology.

Who Is He is who he is, but like the Raven, he is an unknown: he is *who he is going to be.* In part, he is *who we allow him to become.* Like a Haida delegate arriving to negotiate a land claim, or a Haida god arriving in search of a wife, what he can say and teach and mean depends in part on how we receive him.

If he is, as he appears, a Haida aristocrat, some things about him can be known, even before his speech begins. He has ancestors and family, some of whose names we might have heard. And he calls to mind a number of other travelling chiefs and shamans, all out looking for what they have lost. The best known of these are Nanasimgit and Asdiwaal, both sons of gods by human mothers. There are no heroes of greater attainment in Northwest Coast mythology, but the crucial event in the lives of both is the loss of their wives — several times over in Asdiwaal's case. The pain of separation is explored in all its forms in Haida oral literature, and there are countless Orphic stories of lost love — even a few that are sometimes told with happy endings.

I have no doubt at all that the Chief's errand is political: that he is out to save Haida Gwaii from destruction. But the figures swirling around him imply that this is also a deeply personal mission. The Wolf, who is a Raven crest, is sinking his teeth into the Eagle's wing, while the Eagle chews the paw of another Raven crest animal, the Bear. The biting is violent enough to speak of moiety disharmony, implying sexual and cosmic, not merely political, tension. Creatures bite, eat, swallow and disgorge one another everywhere in Haida sculpture; it is one of the ways — almost the only way — in which sexual relations are shown in the visual art. But there is no sign of tenderness in the biting here.

Where is *Who Is He* going? Another big question. And who will he meet, and what will he say when he arrives?

The story of Nanasimgit is told in many sources including The Raven Steals the Light. *The story of Asdiwaal, published by Boas in several versions, is the subject of a well-known study by Claude Lévi-Strauss. See the Suggestions for Further Reading.*

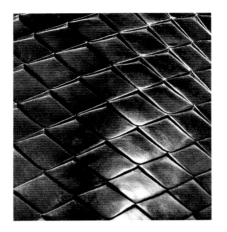

VII

REID, who began his adult life as a poetry-reading radio announcer and his career in the visual arts as a jeweler, has always liked to deliver deceptively simple messages and to work on a deceptively modest physical scale. His monumental sculptures – *The Raven and the First Men*; *Mythic Messengers*; *The Killer Whale* – have all, like the black canoe, grown out of objects you could hold in the palm of your hand. So it is no surprise that some of the inner secrets of *The Spirit of Haida Gwaii* are carried in that modest sculpture-within-a-sculpture held like a chalice in the Chief's hand: the speaker's staff of a silent, close-mouthed man.

At the top of the staff, leaping, is the visible form of the gods, a Killer Whale. Beneath the Whale, wearing the tall hat of wealth with its potlatch rings, is a long-billed Raven. Under the Raven is Ttsaamuus, the Snag, in his Sea Grizzly form. From the Snag's mouth a fourth figure, the Raven once again in fledgling form, has just emerged.

The Whale is the uppermost figure in the canoe, and in an earlier plan for the sculpture, it was one of an unmatched pair. The other was a large, two-dimensional formline Killer Whale that Reid planned to engrave in low relief on the hull. Everyone and everything aboard would then have been carried and cupped between these two. In the end, Reid chose to omit the hull design, and the result is a cleaner, more open-ended form. Graphically, the boat is nameless, echoing the momentary silence of the Chief amidships and the Raven at the helm. The small Whale flies alone at the top of the staff like an understated flag.

The staff is a satisfying composition in itself, handsome in its proportions and resonant with its own internal references and its echoes of other figures in the canoe. It is more satisfying yet if we also recognize – as an earlier Haida audience certainly would have – some of the stories it alludes to and the quotations it contains.

The lower figures – the Raven with the tall hat, and the Sea Grizzly form of the Snag – are precise quotations from an older speaker's staff, now in storage at the Smithsonian Institution, only a few blocks away from the black canoe. The older staff was purchased at Masset by a collector in 1883, and we can be reasonably certain that it was owned and used by Xana of the Skidauqau, Town Mother of Masset in the early nineteenth century, or by an heir laying claim to his power. Museum records tell us nothing of who made or owned the staff or from whom it

was purchased, but the figures from the upper part of the staff match exactly the figures on the upper part of Xana's memorial pole, which was still standing at Masset when the first photographers arrived, more than a century ago.

Xana's heir and successor, his nephew Sigai, departed from Haida custom by naming as his own successor his son, Wiha of the Sghajuughahllaanas of the Eagle side, instead of his nephew Xana the Younger. Some years later, Wiha himself compounded this departure from tradition by consenting to be baptized. Reid's quotation from the elder Xana's staff therefore carries us back to the last generation of traditional rule in the largest settlement in Haida Gwaii. Not to a time before European contact, but to a time when the old social structure was still intact, before European manners, values and religion had established their powerful hold.

The old staff is broken at the bottom, and some of the lower figures are missing. Whether they corresponded to the lower figures on Xana's memorial pole is now impossible to decide. But unlike the pole, the staff is made in two parts, seamlessly fitted. The uppermost figure on the lower section – perhaps a broken-beaked Raven, matching the one on the pole, but just as possibly an Eagle or a Hawk – has a tall hat like the topmost Raven's. This hat forms the peg of the joint that holds the staff together and is therefore invisible while the staff is whole. When the two sections are pulled apart, this tall hat is revealed, asserting the lower bird's claim to stature and wealth coequal with that of the long-beaked Raven above.

If the staff predates the pole, as I think it does, there is little doubt the staff was Xana's. If it postdates the pole, it was carved for his nephew Sigai or for someone else who had reason to evoke Xana's name by alluding to his memorial pole. Reid in any case has quoted only the upper part of the old staff – the portion that clearly represents Xana. In the black canoe, the lower portion of the staff is no more than implied. It is buried in the crowd – or has it simply been discarded and *replaced* by that tumult of creatures? On this reading, Reid the perpetual craftsman and handyman could have built the entire *Spirit of Haida Gwaii* to replace the broken and missing figures from the bottom of Xana's staff.

The other major alteration Reid has made to the old staff is to add the topmost figure, the Killer Whale, which has no counterpart at all on the original. The old forms – long-billed Raven with human hands, perched on the head of the Ttsaamuus – are proudly held aloft, yet they are cupped between the solitary Whale and the populous canoe that are Reid's own.

This is not to say that the chief in the black canoe is Xana. But he seems to have reclaimed Xana's staff from the museum, where it had

Far left, on the facing page: two views of the broken speaker's staff, 82 cm tall, purchased at Masset in 1883. National Museum of Natural History, Smithsonian Institution, Washington, DC. Catalogue no. 88833, Dept of Anthropology. Photos courtesy the Smithsonian Institution.

Near left: Three memorial poles, two frontal poles and a shorter mortuary pole (farthest left in the photograph) seen over the rooftops of Ghadaghaxiwaas (Masset), Haida Gwaii, in 1878. Xana's memorial pole is the tallest of the six. Only the two upper figures – the long-billed Raven and the Snag – are visible in the photograph. Photo by George Dawson. National Archives of Canada, National Photography Collection, PA 38149.

lain for a hundred years. Like Xana, and like Reid, he is also a member of the Raven side. The Snag woven into his dancing blanket, and the Whale, Raven and Snag on his speaker's staff, are all crests of Raven families. But as always in serious Haida art, there is far more going on here than simple heraldic display.

This combination of figures, Raven and Snag, is the most frequent of all themes in Haida sculpture: a theme as ubiquitous as the adoration or the crucifixion in European art, and no less potent once its significance is known.

This story, like those, has many facets and is differently evoked in different contexts. The sexual dimensions of the theme are usually paramount in rattles. On storage boxes and thrones, the same figures differently portrayed speak of perpetual wealth and fecundity, but not in apparently sexual terms. On housepoles, the conjunction of Raven and Snag alludes to the first sharing of this wealth through the creation of the world. Photos from the 1880s confirm that, at the end of the nineteenth century, this same arrangement of figures – Raven above, Snag below – was the most common motif on Haida housepoles of both the Eagle and the Raven sides. It is not impossible that in some earlier age it was the *only* motif on housepoles – because vertically assembled, these figures evoke the original housepole: the stone pole of the Snag, which stood on the floor of the ocean before the creation of Haida Gwaii.

*

This version of the story of creation follows the opening of the Raven epic as told by John Sky of the Qquuna Qiighawaai, with amplifications by Job Moody of the Sttawaas Xhaaidaghaai. In the Swanton archive, the first page of the Haida transcript of this story is missing, though Swanton's English translation of the page survives.

In the morning of the world, there was nothing but water. The Loon was calling, and the old man who at that time bore the Raven's name, Nang-kilstlas, asked her why.

"The gods are homeless," the Loon replied.

"I'll see to it," said the old man, without moving from the fire in his house on the floor of the sea.

Then as the old man continued to lie by his fire, the Raven flew over the sea. The clouds broke. He flew upward, drove his beak into the sky and scrambled over the rim to the upper world. There he discovered a town, and in one of the houses a woman had just given birth.

The Raven stole the skin and form of the newborn child. Then he began to cry for solid food, but he was offered only mother's milk. That night, he passed through the town stealing an eye from each inhabitant. Back in his foster parents' house, he roasted the eyes in the coals and ate them, laughing. Then he returned to his cradle, full and warm.

He had not seen the old woman watching him from the corner – the one who never slept and who never moved because she was stone from the waist down. Next morning, amid the wailing that engulfed the town, she told what she had seen. The one-eyed people of the sky

64

dressed in their dancing clothes, paddled the child out to mid-heaven in their canoe and pitched him over the side.

He turned round and round to the right as he fell from the sky back to the water. Still in his cradle, he floated on the sea. Then he bumped against something solid.

"Your illustrious grandfather asks you in," said a voice. The Raven saw nothing. He heard the same words again, and then again, but still he saw nothing but water. Then he peered through the hole in his marten-skin blanket. Beside him was a grebe.

"Your illustrious grandfather asks you in," said the grebe, and dived.

Level with the waves beside him, the Raven discovered the top of a housepole made of stone. He untied himself from his cradle and climbed down the pole to the lowermost figure.

Hala qaattsi ttakkin-gha, a voice said: "Come inside, my grandson."

Behind the fire, at the rear of the house, was an old man white as a gull.

"I have something to lend you," said the old man. "I have something to tell you as well. *Dii hau dang iiji*: I am you."

Slender bluegreen things with wings were moving between the screens at the back of the house. *Waa'asing dang iiji*, said the old man again: "That also is you."

The old man gave the Raven two small sticks, like gambling sticks, one black, one multicolored. He gave him instructions to bite them apart in a certain way and told him to spit the pieces at one another on the surface of the sea.

The Raven climbed back up the pole, where he promptly did things backwards, just to see if something interesting would occur, and the pieces bounced apart. It may well be some bits were lost. But when he gathered what he could and tried again – and this time followed the instructions he had been given – the pieces stuck and rumpled and grew to become the mainland and Haida Gwaii.

*

Like everything else in the living world – like his counterpart or double Nangdldastlas, for example – the old man on the floor of the sea, who is the Raven's titular grandfather, requires reincarnation from time to time. He grows old and needs a successor. Important pieces of his story are missing from the early records, waiting for another Haida poet who chooses to record them, but we have some of the salient details. One of the old man's names is Taangghwanlaana, the One in the Sea.

Henry Moody of the Qaagyals Qiighawaai, who was John Swanton's interpreter at Skidegate, mentioned one day that when the Snag spoke through a shaman, it was the same as if the Raven himself had spoken.

Above: a Chilkat blanket, of mountain goat hair and yellowcedar bark, by an unidentified weaver, 19th century, 91 × 167 cm excluding the fringe (American Museum of Natural History). Below: a bracelet of gold and fossil ivory by Bill Reid, 1964, 5.3 cm wide (from a private collection). Both of these garments – the large one in wool and the small one in metal – are representations of the hide of Tsaghanxuuwaji, the Sea Grizzly, who is a form of the Ttsaamuus or Snag. One who wears the hide of this animal announces his own (or a male relative's) prowess as a hunter and also a willingness to take on the role of the Ttsaamuus, supporting the world. Blanket photo: neg. no. 323235, courtesy Dept of Library Services, American Museum of Natural History.

And from another of the old storytellers, Swanton learned that the Snag sometimes slept with Taangghwanlaana's wife, who was the Creek Woman of Guudal.

In the language of Haida myth, this second piece of gossip suggests that the Snag is Taangghwanlaana's nephew and heir. If Taangghwanlaana is literally the Raven's paternal grandfather, and the Snag is Taangghwanlaana's sister's son, he is also the Raven's mother's brother, and it fits together snugly: three generations of males who all belong to the Raven side. Each is entitled to say to the other, *I am you.*

That is one among several interpretations. There is evidence that some of the nineteenth-century carvers and storytellers collapsed these figures into the span of two generations: the Snag, and his titular grandson or nephew the Raven. This simplifies everything, but it doesn't quite leave room for the ramifications of the myths explored by poets like John Sky and carvers like Charles Edenshaw.

The Raven, in any case, is the most prodigal of nephews. He can't inherit the Snag's position, because the Raven has other business in the upper world. The Snag is replaced or rejuvenated instead by heroes who from time to time capture one of his incarnations, either the Seawolf or Sea Grizzly, enter its skin, and take up residence under the sea, at the base of the pole. Chilkat blankets often hint at this act of bravado. Many of these blankets represent the skin of the Killer Whale, the archetypal form of the gods. Many others – like the one Reid has created for the Chief in the black canoe – portray the Seawolf's or Sea Grizzly's hide. The man who wears such a dancing blanket impersonates the hero who captures the Seawolf and enters the sea in its skin – and who for a time thereby becomes the prince of wealth and the chief, or heir to the chief, of the Killer Whales.

The story of such a hero has been preserved, once again in the voice of the poet John Sky of the Qquuna Qiighawaai, from Reid's ancestral village of Tanu.

After bathing for strength in his mother's house and showing his sister his skills as a seahunter, a young man tested himself in private against several powerful creatures. From one, he obtained a strand of kelp – the supernatural creature's hair – which he wore thereafter as a headband. He received important advice from the Mouse Woman, and further advice from the Wren. Thus equipped, he was able to trap and skin the Waasghu or Seawolf. Then he came upon a house, at Xaina in Skidegate Inlet, where he had not seen one before.

> *Tajxwaa giina qquudlxiwas,*
> *xhiitgu nang taighaaghudyis.*
> *Ghiista ghulaamalagundyisi.*

Chilkat blankets are so called after the Chilkat River – only one of many locations where some of the early examples were made. In Haida as in Tlingit, such a garment is called naaxiin. In the Tsimshian country, where the form may have originated, it is called gwusnaigmgyaamk.

Here, for once, the word supernatural may be appropriate. Sky's stories, like the black canoe itself, are not without their elements of fantasy or metaphysical play – yet they contain scarcely a single word or image that doesn't contribute to their analysis of the real and natural world.

Wagu xaltsipdagadyisi.
La qindi qaudi wasta xalghadlixasi.
Tajxwi sghaanaqidas taixyindyas.

At the rear of the house something hung down.
Beneath it, one lay facing upward.
Flames hissed and licked from it.
Also it sizzled.
As he watched, that one was driven out by the fire.
In the rear of the house the gods were gathered around.

The young man, still nameless at this stage, has come upon a gathering of the gods who are seeking a replacement for the Seawolf he has killed.

The Seawolf's position cannot remain vacant, because he serves as the living foundation for the pole that holds up the world – though the poet's language sometimes suggests that there is such a pole, and a Seawolf or Seabear beneath it, for every inhabited island, rather than one for the entirety of Haida Gwaii.

Reincarnating the Seawolf involves reallocating the places of the gods. The nameless hero of the story finds them discussing where they will settle, as if they were faced with the recreation of the world. And some of the beings at this gathering are nervous that the dead Seawolf – a member of the Raven side – may now be replaced by an Eagle. In the context of this rivalry, some salacious gossip arises concerning the conduct of Jilaquns, the Raven's wife. She and her descendants belong, of course, to the Eagle side (and so, by the way, did John Sky, who crafted and performed the only full recorded version of this story). Jilaquns is present at the gathering, and her son, Ghudangxhiiwat, has entered to be tested for the Seawolf's position. Many of those assembled are therefore clamoring for a contender from the Raven side.

One of Jilaquns' lovers was sent for, to weaken Ghudangxhiiwat by embarrassing his mother. Just before dawn on the fourth and final day of the test, Jilaquns's son was driven out by the heat of the pole.

Wiyadhau ttl gudaxungdi
qaudi nang gyaaxhattlxas han siiwus,
"Quyaagyaaghandaal ttla taanghaghu.
Lahau l xiitgu tsyagai ghan agang gin-gha ttl suughan."

Then they gave it thought.
Then someone stood up and said,
"Quyaagyaaghandaal ought to be sent for.
He bathed in the sea in order to settle beneath it, they say."

Hearing these words, the young man recognized his role. *Quyaagyaaghandaal* means "Honored, Standing, Travelling." The hunter returned home and called his mother and sister to join him. Dressed in his Seawolf skin, standing amidships and travelling in his canoe while his mother steered and his sister sat in the bow, he arrived back at the gathering of the gods, enacting his new name. With his sister's aid, he passed the test and took up his place as the living root of the world. *Gyanhau sghaanaqiidas gaghei tsyaasas uu kilghuhlghayas ghei agang dangadigas Xainalnagai sta a*: "Then those born as gods went out to settle in the places they had chosen, leaving the town of Xaina behind."

*

A linked series of stories ties the theme of cosmic lovemaking to the story of Quyaagyaaghandaal, and there is a wealth of visual evidence linking the images of the Raven and the Snag with sexual rapture as well. In the stories, some of the lovemaking takes place in canoes. In the visual art, lovers — one by one or both in one — are carried across the *xhaaidla* on the Raven's back: flown, it appears, to the floor of the sea, where for a moment perhaps they too are conjunct with the source of all the wealth in the world. This theme is strongest in that ubiquitous, beautiful object the raven rattle, once used on ceremonial occasions all over the Northwest Coast.

A human being lies in a sexual posture on the Raven's back, and the genital face in the tail of the Raven rises up in the form of another bird. This bird itself, or a frog that it holds in its beak, shares a tongue with the semi-prone human. In the Raven's breast is the face of the Snag. In use, the rattle is held to the side with the Snag facing upward. The Raven and his enraptured human cargo fly upside-down.

When the same figures, Raven and Snag, share the exterior of a box, as they frequently do, the Snag in his full symmetrical glory takes over the sides while the Raven is assigned the ends. The Raven is usually drawn asymmetrically, schematically and in transformation: reduced, for instance, to a human face and a wing, or to a few calligraphic gestures more abstract than that. This is the painterly way of saying what one says about the Raven: "It's the one it usually is."

When the same figures appear together on a pole, they are often elaborated with other intriguing details. First, the young Raven is often shown emerging from the Snag's mouth and resting on his belly. This is the sculptural equivalent of Henry Moody's statement that the Snag's voice and the Raven's voice are the same, and the sculptor's answer to the mythteller's statement, *Dii hau dang iiji*: "I am you." Second, the adult Raven above the Snag is often equipped with fingers or hands, as a sign of his position on the *xhaaidla*, in transition between human and

avian forms. Third, the Raven's beak is often abnormally prolonged — with the result that the Raven in this position has often been misidentified as the Cormorant or the Heron.

In Xana's staff, and in the larger version held by the Chief in the black canoe, all these details are present. A young Raven is emerging from the Sea Grizzly's mouth, and fingers are visible under the long beak of the adult Raven above. The fingers are subtle, and the carver who executed these figures on Xana's memorial pole was confronted with a decision. He had to exaggerate the fingers into hands, to make them perceptible from the ground, or omit them altogether. By taking the latter course, he was able to keep the original conformation of the figure. When Reid first modelled the staff in clay and carved it in plaster, he also omitted the fingers — and the young Raven as well — either because he thought they would clutter a staff that could only be viewed from a distance, or because they did not coincide with his vision. But something about the form displeased him. It was only then that he commissioned Don Yeomans to carve the staff again in yellowcedar and furnished Yeomans with photographs of Xana's staff from the Smithsonian collection as a guide. Yeomans carved the figures less deeply, while adding some beautiful surface carving on the backs and tails, but he chose to copy all the transformational features — the fingers, the small Raven, the fins and feet of the Seabear — which are present on the older staff.

It was not the young Raven's ambition, in the morning of the world, that led him to create the mainland and Haida Gwaii. It was his grandfather who summoned him, because the Loon's call reminded him that the gods required shelter. There were no human beings in those days. The Raven had not discovered them. It was the gods, not humans, who needed forests, mountains, streams, seacliffs, beaches, reefs and lakes, as well as open ocean. That world, into which human beings were born, was created out of the Old Man's thought and the Raven's action. In John Sky's story, it is recreated anew by Quyaagyaaghandaal when he takes the Snag's place at the base of the pole.

Between the Snag and the Raven, who both rest there in the hand of the standing and travelling Chief, the black canoe carries more than the power to come to land. It carries a sign of the deep fecundity of being and a memory of creation. It even carries a reminder and a clue to how the world might be remade, if the gods should lose their places or surface people in their greed should sweep them entirely away. Overtly stated, such a claim would be as arrogant and specious as the claims of Ozymandias. Wordlessly, in miniature, carried like seed in the fruit, concealed in the speaker's staff held by a silent man in the midst of a motionless canoe, it is one of the secret truths of the myths, and of *The Spirit of Haida Gwaii.*

On the facing page are two Raven rattles, Tlingit (above) and Tsimshian (below), by unidentified 19th-century carvers. The overall form is that of the Raven. In his belly is the face of the Snag. The Raven's tail and genitals take the form of another bird, either long-billed or curl-billed, and a human being reclines on the Raven's back.

In many such rattles, the tailbird faces to the rear, in others forward. A frog is also usually included, sometimes perched on the human's chest or between his legs, and sometimes held in the beak of the tailbird. As a rule either the frog or the tailbird itself shares a tongue with the recumbent human being. More rarely (as in the upper rattle on the facing page, though it is invisible in the photograph) the frog is perched on the face of the Snag. The Snag himself is usually also equipped with a lower face whose erect, protruding tongue becomes the handle by which the rattle is held.

Among other variations on the raven rattle theme, there are examples in which the Raven's upraised tail is replaced by the killer whale tail of the Snag, and the frog by a bent killer whale fin emerging from the Raven's back. Raven/ Killer Whale rhymes are frequent in Northwest Coast art, as are portrayals of a human being (usually Nanasimget's wife) being abducted by the Killer Whale. Like the black canoe itself, whale-tailed raven rattles embody not a single story but a compound image in which several stories intersect.

Photos: neg. no. 2A12676 (above) and 338131 (below), courtesy Dept of Library Services, American Museum of Natural History.

On the facing page: part of the complex of poles and houses built by Reid and his assistant, Doug Cranmer, at the University of British Columbia, 1958–62.

The principal figure on the memorial pole in the foreground is a Beaver holding a stick in his forepaws. There is a human face in his tail and a Bear Cub perched within and between his ears. The other two-thirds of the pole, not visible in the photograph, are occupied by the Beaver's very tall hat (which is the axis of the world and an emblem of the Beaver's wealth and generosity) with a Raven (the self-centred but effective distributor of that wealth) perched at the crown.

On the housepole in the background there are two subjects or thematic groupings, and the boundary between them coincides with the roof of the house.

From the top of the pole, the figures are as follows. (1) Three watchmen are perched on the head of (2) the Raven, who has human arms. In the Raven's feathered tail is (3) a human face with a spawning-salmon nose, alluding simultaneously to his sexuality and to his alternate human form. The Raven is standing with his feet in the ears of (3) Ttsaamuus, the Snag, in Seabear form. As the Snag is the Raven's grandfather or uncle, he carries (4) the baby Raven on his chest. The Seabear in turn is seated on (5) another denizen of the deep sea, the Frog, who is sharing a tongue with (6) the tiny human face between his looming, circular eyes. This sequence of figures – the entire first subject of the pole, apart from the three watchmen – is, in effect, a Raven rattle in columnar form.

The second subject is built around a single large figure, (7) a Grizzly, who has (8) a Bear cub perched in and between his ears as well as (9) a Frog emerging from his mouth, in pursuit of (10) a small Wolf with his tail between his legs. Perhaps for visibility, the tail is shown along the Wolf's back rather than his belly.

Both poles have nineteenth-century precursors: a memorial pole from Skidegate and a housepole from Sghan-gwaai. (These are Skidegate 1M and Ninstints 12 in George MacDonald's catalogue.)

The housepole, which follows its source almost verbatim, is the only one of the five Reid carved for the University of British Columbia that could sensibly be called a copy. The original of this pole, probably carved around 1800, belonged to a chief named Qinaga'istl, "Heavyweight," of the Ghangxhit Qiighawaai, of the Eagle side. It had fallen by 1901. The disintegrating pieces were removed from Sghan-gwaii to Vancouver in 1957.

Except for the Frog, none of the creatures on this pole is a known crest of Qinaga'istl or his family. The family's claim to the Frog may help to explain its prominence here at the centre of the pole, but the figures assert something older and deeper than heraldry. The upper group alludes to the Raven's creation of the surface world around the original stone housepole of the snag. The lower group alludes to the transformation of that world through the redistribution of power among its inhabitants, including human beings. In this process, the first bonds were formed between humans and other animals, through marriage and adoption, and certain giant animals – Beaver and Grizzly in particular – were transformed from their original size and ferocity to forms less threatening to humankind. On the Northwest Coast, the agent of transformation in such stories takes a multitude of forms. It is sometimes the Raven, the Wren or the Wolf, or a consortium of these, and sometimes a hybrid being whose animal form is that of the Beaver, the Bear or the Dog. The Frog, who is in almost every respect the inverse of the Bear, is also often mentioned or displayed in such a context, not as the agent but as the fulcrum of transformation.

The precursor of the memorial pole, carved in 1882, lacked the classical grace of Reid's version. Reid was drawn to the old pole nevertheless, perhaps because it was the only one still standing in his mother's village in the 1950s.

Details of the yellowcedar pattern for the Chief's staff, carved by Don Yeomans, after the original in the Smithsonian Institution. The figures are the Raven with human hands, and the Ttsaamuus or Snag in the form of a Seabear (Grizzly with finned arms and a killer whale's tail). The young Raven is emerging from the Snag's mouth.

VIII

AS AN IMAGE of latter-day Haida culture – figures from a fallen totem pole and characters from the stories of a strangled language gathered like mythological Boat People into that mother of forms, the canoe – *The Spirit of Haida Gwaii* is remarkably self-contained. But the sea in which it travels is full of other echoes tying the work to the larger world. Reid himself delights in making some of these connections – pointing out after-the-fact allusions to A.A. Milne and Carl Sandburg, for example, or a tongue-in-cheek resemblance to Emanuel Leutze's portrait of *Washington Crossing the Delaware*.

Some equally interesting contrasts also come to mind. Proud and assertive though he is, this Chief shares his canoe with two women, another man and nine distinctly undomesticated animals. It is the Raven, with the Mouse Woman's whispered advice, who is steering the boat; the Chief himself is not in control. He has something in common with that small Etruscan bronze in which Romulus and Remus are suckled by a wolf, but he is twelve times removed from two prototypical subjects of more recent European public sculpture: the crucified man, whose doctrine of brotherly love has been answered with torture and jeers, and the hero on horseback: the Colleoni or Napoleon or Pizarro, who trumpets his and his nation's preeminence over all other creatures and cultures.

I think of another boat as well, that sits in public space in front of another embassy in another major capital, yet seems to differ from this canoe in every way. It is Pietro Bernini's little vessel in the Piazza di Spagna in Rome. The animal images it contains – the Barberini family's bees – are heraldry alone, with hardly a shred of mythology left. Bernini's boat is white instead of black, and full of ruminative sighs instead of embryonic speeches. And though the tourists crowd upon it by the thousands, it is resolutely empty: an abandoned ship, simultaneously melting and sinking into its pool.

The black canoe is Noah's Ark and Cook's *Endeavour*, the flagship of a culture, and Huck and Jim's disintegrating raft. A cargo ship and lifeboat, bearing the treasures of prehistory; a shaman and his familiars on their voyage under the sky's rim; a diplomatic mission from an almost vanished nation to the reigning power of the hemisphere; and an exploratory vessel, sailing an unknown course through unknown seas. Beings looking for other beings to speak to, feast with, trade with, perhaps to intermarry with, not for a place to plant a flag.

And it is one lone Indian, evidently, from a vanished era, cooling his heels here on the embassy's doorstep, waiting for a visa from the nation-state that now lays claim to his home.

But if these are the ghosts leaving Tanu, where are they bound? Are they paddling to Byzantium, where goldsmiths cage the souls of weary men in the forms of immortal birds? Or is Byzantium – that serenely oblivious capital of a bygone empire – where they have in fact arrived?

Once, Reid returned from his annual pilgrimage to the Islands saying the ghosts had left at last; his grandmother's village was finally empty. The next year, shaking his head, he said they were back again. In his mind, I believe, these creatures are not so much gathered aboard the canoe as they are grown out of it. The Haida canoe is not to him, nor to anyone else who has made one, something as simple as a hollowed log prized open to serve as container and conveyance. It is the original vulvic form, the delicate source and fruit of taut exactitude, and the womb from which Haida art, myth, technology and character were born. It is the other side of entirety, which answers back to the Snag's pole and to all the phallic columns in the world: the sculptural pillars of Haida Gwaii, Egyptian obelisks, the towering structures of Paris and New York, and the Washington Monument, just up the road. A lifeboat it may be, but it is the living womb as well, the warm and fertile mouth of thought and being. The creatures of Haida myth are reemerging from it now, before our eyes. And the silent speaker, wearing the hide of a god, is riding in that canoe down to the floor of the sea, for a moment at least, to take up the weight of the world.

They are arriving, not departing. Perhaps, in fact, they are returning to Haida Gwaii.

They are also going nowhere, as all of us always are, because all the worlds are one and there is nothing but this moment and this planet to explore. Perhaps it is not a boat at all, moored in its little pool, but an overpopulated island.

It is also another embassy, just outside Big Brother's, with a stony-faced ambassador of its own. The entire black canoe is to Arthur Erickson's building, which surrounds it like an opened box, as the Chief's staff is to the loaded canoe. It is a sculpture within a sculpture, a locked container of meaning – but locked as the myths are, closed and yet wide open.

In John Sky's story of creation, the black and (probably) copper-colored objects from which the Raven creates the mainland and the Islands are kept in a concentric nest of boxes. Five in all, Sky says. Reid, telling similar stories, prefers to speak of an infinite number of boxes. Here, like medieval theologians, we can count to almost any chosen number the concentric rings of proud yet fragile power enclosing the spirit of *The Spirit of Haida Gwaii*: the old staff in the new staff, wrapped in the hand of the Chief who stands in the boat that is moored in a tiny patch of Canadian ground, surrounded by the U S A. Myth surrounded by history, surrounded by the stretch of the present day, which is surrounded in its turn, perhaps by the history and myth it purports to contain.

Reid is apt to say that the piece as a whole is derived from nothing more than memories of taking the family for Sunday drives – dogs and children lunging at one another across the station-wagon seats while mother stares out placidly and father resolutely at the road. This sort of Raven-like understatement suits him well, and would serve in a world where the forms and their meanings were common knowledge. In such a world, those who wished to see only a pleasant play of forms would find it; those who looked for the weave of meaning over the sharp knife of the truth would see that too. But such a homogeneous world no longer exists – not in the rich, polluted capitals of Europe and North America, and not in the remote and plundered landscape of the Amazon, Tibet or Haida Gwaii. Artists apprenticed to anything more than fashion now send signals using what tools they have at hand, no longer knowing who is out there to receive.

Construed in the terms of Haida social grammar, the canoe is as perfectly balanced as canoes must always be. Eagle, Beaver and Frog are crests of the Eagle side; Killer Whale, Grizzly and Wolf of the Raven side; and the Raven and Dogfish are claimed by families on both sides. The Mouse Woman is no one's crest. The unilateral crests are forward and amidships, linked in a chain around the Chief, while the bilateral crests are aft. Under the Raven crouches his grandmother the Mouse Woman. Under the Eagle crouches that other ancient creature, his crest sister the Frog. The elegance of this arrangement is considerable and considered. It is Reid's homage to his Haida forebears and nameless, improbable heirs – for he knows that those who see the sculpture now will neither recall the arcane details nor comprehend the inner meaning of the old heraldic system. It is nothing so nostalgic or ingrown as family pride.

Most of these unilateral crests – Wolf and Eagle, Beaver and Bear – are also crests of the white man, and Reid is too sly to forget that, as well as too honest to let this knowledge turn the head of Haida tradition. Washingtonians and diplomats will make what they choose of the fact that the Bear is sailing bare-assed and backwards into the future while the Eagle is biting his hand, and the hungry Wolf is arching over the loaded canoe with his claws in the Beaver's ample back and his teeth in the thin flesh of the Eagle's wing.

Artists at home in the white tradition have imported Native American themes into their works for a good many years — at least since Longfellow's *Hiawatha* and Antonin Dvořák's "Indian Quintet." Farther along on a parallel road, there are artists like Bartók, Yeats and Stravinsky, who have brought to the churning clock of imperial fashion not only themes but forms, concepts and values from indigenous traditions to which they had privileged access. Reid is one of their peers: a mediator not only between two art traditions but between two worlds. And Reid has taken a very substantial further step, possible in the visual arts where it seemed not to be in music or in literature. He has rooted his art solidly in a prehistoric, Native American tradition, though he continues to live and work in the white world. That little byplay with the Wolf, the American Eagle and Smokey or Igor or Grandfather Bear makes the difference clear. Reid can now do Dvořák's and Longfellow's trick in reverse. He can, for informative amusement, lace a white colonial theme into a solidly aboriginal composition.

Like Haida hunters and artists of earlier centuries, Reid moves back and forth across a boundary, fastidious in his technique, respectfully silent concerning his prey. The boundary has shifted slightly; the *xhaaidla* rests now between the stone age and the machine age, between the tribal and colonized world. It lies between prehistory and history — but as always, between two kinds of time. The land itself, the animals in the land, and the animals of the spirit live, as they always did, on one side, where the ancestors have joined them. Here on the other side are the audience, the sponsorships and commissions, the medical diagnoses, the logging trucks and political confrontations. They remain, to borrow a newer Canadian metaphor, two solitudes, two cultures.

Many — I want to say all — serious artists confront such a boundary as a condition of their working lives. Some use that boundary for a mirror. Many cross as visitors, returning with their photographs, impressions, souvenirs. Reid, like the Dogfish Woman and the Bear Mother, now has citizenship and family and heritage and a kind of language on both sides.

Once in Haida Gwaii, between the surface world and the deep worlds of forest, sea and sky, a remarkably delicate and firm balance existed. Each side sought to consume and digest the other, and each nourished the other. For perhaps thirty centuries, this balance was preserved. In the two hundred years of its absence, much has changed. Reid, in his work, has reasserted it: set an ancient principle to work in altered terms.

The boundary between these worlds — prehistory and history, mythtime and surface time — is the surface on which he works. And the two worlds now interpenetrate completely. The surface arcs and folds, driving him to work in three dimensions. Reid crosses that boundary and returns, but he brings no souvenirs. Anything that crosses with him is necessarily changed. He brings it to the surface, like the mythcreature whose hide becomes a Chilkat blanket, or the Dogfish Woman confronting her husband after the years of separation. He brings it to the boundary, where its absolute otherness can be touched and seen.

The deepest instinct of Haida culture is that there must always be two sides, and that they must come together in marriage: that they must touch: that the boundary between them must be crossed repeatedly – and that the boundary nevertheless is absolute and must remain.

Seen with one eye, *The Spirit of Haida Gwaii* still fits the imperial paradigm. Here once again are the exotic treasures of the provinces shipped to the capital for display – like all the totem poles already in museum collections in Ottawa, Paris, New York, as well as Washington, DC. Seen with the other eye, the black canoe replies with quiet Haida eloquence to the tides of power and fortune that brought it where it is. The game of being cowboys and Indians, fur traders and savages, missionaries and heathens, has run its lethal course. These creatures alone are privileged to be in this boat. But all of us now are aground on the same earth and afloat on the same ocean.

THE

PHOTOGRAPHIC

RECORD

JUNE & JULY 1986: Reid at work on the clay sketch. In the earlier version, at left, the Frog is on top of the heap, just forward of the Chief's head. A month later, above, the Frog has found his ultimate place at the gunwale on the starboard bow, but is facing astern. The Raven has acquired considerable definition from one photo to the next, while his close companion, the Ancient Reluctant Conscript, has grown more amorphous.

JULY 1986: Work continues on the clay sketch. At this stage Qqaaxhadajaat, the Dogfish Woman, is a bodiless mask. The Frog has turned part way round, the heads of the Eagle and the Bear Father have shifted position, and the head of the Chief has been momentarily replaced by a portrait bust of Reid himself, made by a visiting friend.

OCTOBER 1986: The plaster model, cast from the clay. The Raven has much of his formline detail, but the Eagle remains vague. As the sculpture developed, Reid often likened the tensions in his boatload of mythcreatures to those of a family outing. "Sunday Afternoon on Lost Lagoon" became one of his nicknames for the piece. The bystander in diplomatic uniform, far left, was constructed in paper to show the ultimate scale. The words in the balloon above his head are "Oh, my God."

At right, JANUARY 1987: Reid has carved away both the Bear Mother's upper body and the Beaver's head, and is replacing the plaster with fresh clay.

18 FEBRUARY 1988: The clay prototype, built at actual size over an armature of steel rod and mesh, is taking shape. At left, Reid with his assistant and project engineer, George Rammell, beside the large clay face of the Beaver. Below, Reid is reshaping the Beaver's left eye.

18 FEBRUARY 1988: The superstructure is still in rough clay, but the plaster mold of the hull is already complete.

The Reluctant Conscript is flanked by the larger figures of the Raven and the Wolf. Rough sketches of the formlines are visible in the Raven's face and wing.

Above, a view of the port side, including the Bear family, the Beaver, and the Dogfish Woman. George Rammell is working on the armature behind the Beaver's head. Reid's pencil sketch of the Beaver is tacked to the Bear Mother's arm. (This maidenly version of the Bear Mother, scaled up from the model, was soon replaced, while the Dogfish Woman, whose face here is heavy-lidded and harsh, passed through other and slower metamorphoses of her own.)

4 APRIL 1988: The Bear family is nearing the end of the clay prototype stage. At this point the Wolf had a plumed tail, which he carried erect. The rough clay version of the Chief's staff is surmounted by a metal armature prefiguring the small Killer Whale that will eventually ride there. On the facing page, 6 APRIL 1988: a closer view of the Bear Mother and the Good Cub.

11 APRIL 1988: The Dogfish Woman and other figures in the stern are still in clay, but the Bear family, at left, is temporarily vanishing into contained space, making the transition from clay prototype to plaster mold.

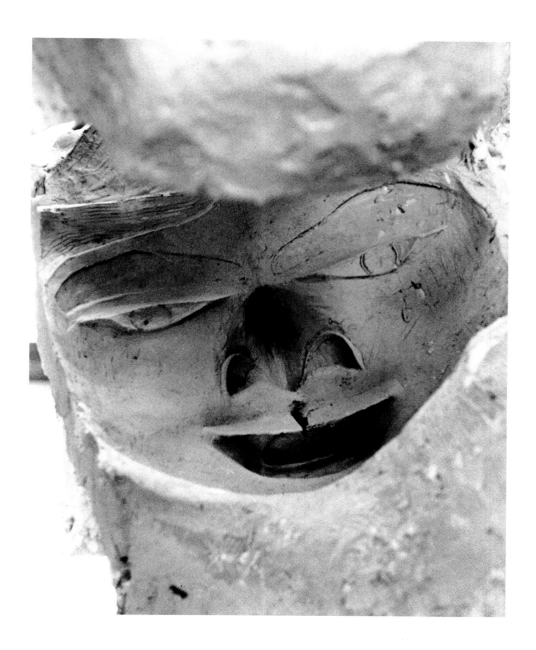

10 MAY 1988: At left is the starboard bow of the completed plaster mold. Through openings in the mold, the clay and its armature have been removed. Some of the lids which fit these openings are visible, piled against the wall behind the mold. Higher on the wall is part of a sketch of the Killer Whale design once planned for the hull of the canoe. The negative image of the Dogfish Woman's face, above, can be seen from within the plaster mold.

10 OCTOBER & 4 NOVEMBER 1988: The cast plaster patterns of the Bear, the Eagle and the Frog, at left, and of the Bear Mother and Cubs, above, are emerging from the plaster mold. The seam marks on the Bear Mother's face and arm betray the sections of the mold.

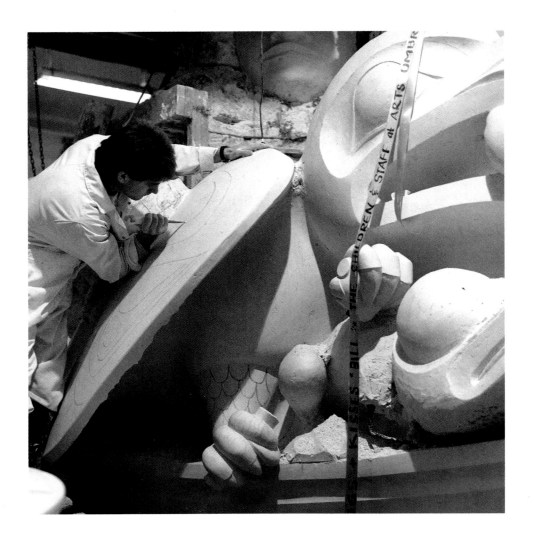

12 JANUARY 1989: Doug Zilkie, a member of Reid's crew, above, engraves the ovoid and formline Reid has laid out on the Eagle's wing.

9 FEBRUARY 1989: At right, George Rammell emerges among the myth-creatures after a session at work on the modular armature he designed and constructed to support the plaster pattern.

101

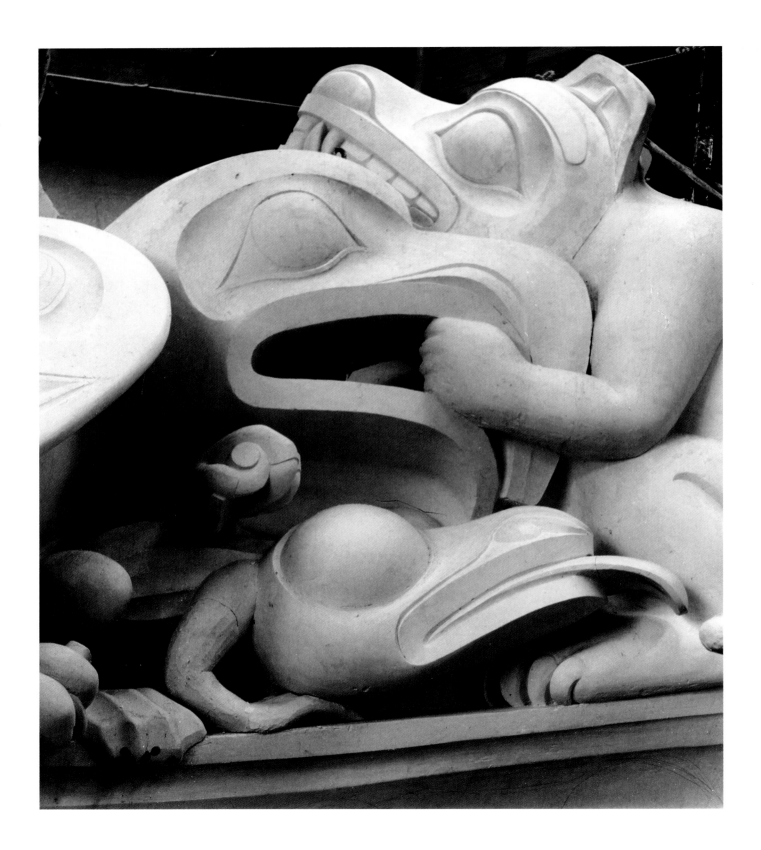

9 FEBRUARY 1989: Many of the figures are still unresolved, but after nearly three years' work, the smooth, tense surfaces and the interlocking forms of Eagle, Frog and Bear, on the opposite page, are nearing the intensity of completion.

16 MARCH 1989: The inscrutably smiling face on this page is that of the Bad Cub, clutching his father's arm.

16 MARCH 1989: The Ancient Reluctant Conscript and his guardian figure, the Raven, on the facing page, are under steady revision.

25 MARCH 1989: The Conscript, who has many of Reid's facial features, acquires Doug Zilkie's shoulders and knees. Reid tried posing as his own model for the Ancient Reluctant, but the only available cedarbark cape was too small for him. Zilkie, who worked on the sculpture primarily as a plaster finisher, fit the garment perfectly and the combination of models fit the convention of Haida sculpture, in which the head is routinely carved to a larger scale than the body.

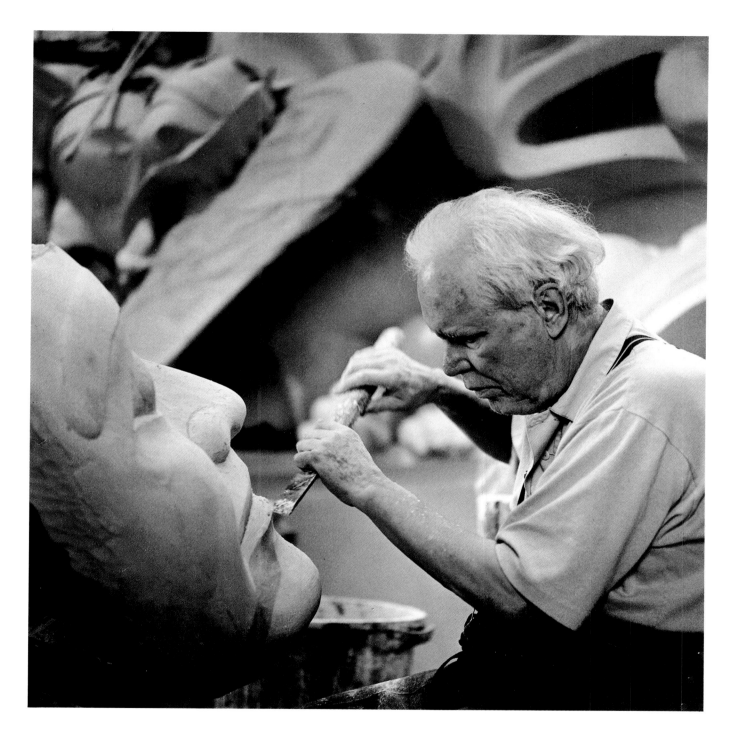

5 APRIL 1989: George Rammell laying up plaster for the Conscript's cape; Reid shaving plaster from the Chief's face.

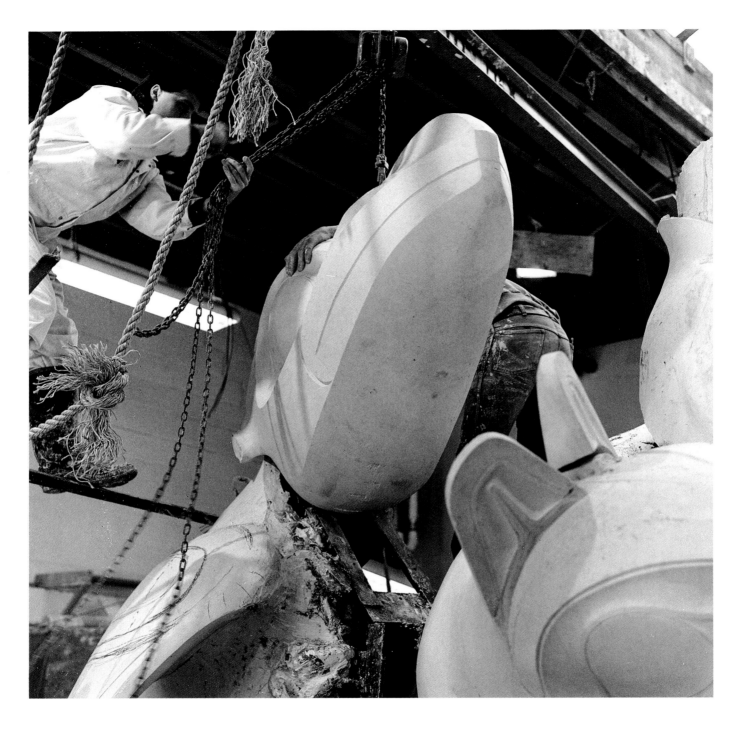

19 APRIL 1989: Refitting the edited heads of the Raven and the Dogfish Woman. Reid has sketched a new ovoid and formline pattern on the Raven's reproportioned wing.

109

26 APRIL 1989: Rammell with two other members of the crew, James Watt and John Nutter, installing the Chief's hat.

17 JUNE 1989: One of the Wolf's hind feet is tabled for close inspection.

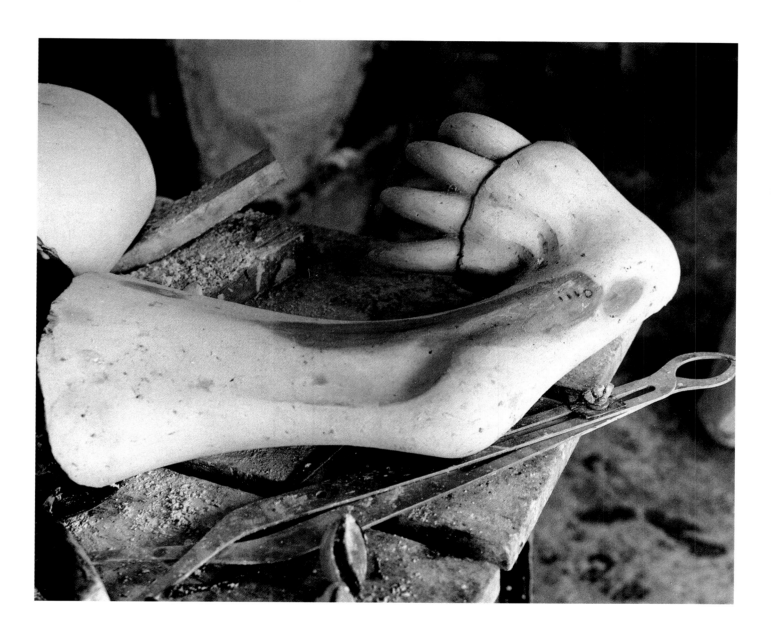

24 MAY 1989: Doug Zilkie checking symmetry and proportions in the Bear
Mother's face, and Nancy Brignall at
work on the Chief's cape.

22 JUNE 1989: The Chief in his hat and cape.

26 JUNE 1989: Qaganjaat, the Mouse Woman, still with feet of clay, emerging beneath the Raven's tail. The formline pattern has been added to the Raven's wings and tail, and his back and legs have been fully fledged.

5 JULY 1989: Rammell thinning the Bear Mother's lip.

19 JULY 1989: Qqaaxhadajaat, the Dogfish Woman, with her vertical pupils, curled nose, gill slits and labret.

(Archaeological research suggests that the labret – a plug in the perforated lower lip – was once worn by Haida of both sexes. In historical times, it was worn only by high-caste women.)

5 JULY 1989: The port bow of the plaster pattern. The Chief's staff, with its Killer Whale finial, is now in plaster, but the Wolf's tail and the Bear Mother's left hand are out for revision.

12 JULY 1989: Reid with a small adze making further revisions to the plaster pattern of the little Killer Whale.

119

14 JULY 1989: Bow and stern of the largely completed plaster pattern. George Rammell stands at the starboard side of the sculpture, above. Behind him is a duplicate plaster cast of the Bear Mother's head.

14 JULY 1989: All hands on watch. Here, in the stern, Qqaaxhadajaat, the Dogfish Woman, and Qaganjaat, the Mouse Woman, are looking fore and aft. Between them is an ovoid face, known to Northwest Coast carvers as a salmon-trout head, looking out from the Raven's shoulder. Opposite, in the bow, the Bear family is grouped around the Eagle's eye.

19 JULY 1989: Both ends of the Wolf, with some of his companions. The Wolf's tail is close to its final shape but has none of its final texture.

22 JULY 1989 & 3 AUGUST 1989: Reid
still at work on the faces of the Mouse
Woman and the Ancient Reluctant
Conscript.

1

2

3

4   5

QQAAXHADAJAAT, the Dogfish Woman, in some of her
sequential incarnations.

(1) JULY 1986: the peaceful mask of the clay model;

(2) 18 FEBRUARY 1988: the heavy-lidded eyes, gill-slit tiara
and swept-back hair of the first clay prototype;

(3) 9 NOVEMBER 1988: another clay revision;

(4) 12 JANUARY 1989: the round eyes and smooth cheeks of
the early plaster pattern.

(5) 19 JULY 1989: the vertical eyes and gill-slit cheeks of the
final plaster version.

1

2

3

4

A few of the many transformations of QAGANJAAT, the Mouse Woman.

(1) 5 NOVEMBER 1988: the rough clay prototype. (Part of the pattern gauge, used to scale up the canoe from the small plaster model to the large clay, is visible in the background.)

(2) 14 JULY 1989: the Mouse Woman in peasant dress. The basic figure was plaster at this stage, but Reid was reworking several parts in clay. Apart from its value as cross-cultural costume, the scarf preserved the moisture in the clay. (This photo also shows the alternative means of propulsion which the plaster pattern carried for several months before it left Reid's studio: a blue plastic propeller.)

(3) 10 AUGUST 1989: the rough plaster removed for further revision;

(4) 21 AUGUST 1989: the Mouse Woman reinstalled beneath the half-dismantled Raven.

11 AUGUST 1989: Reid is still face-to-face with the Conscript,
while the Raven is ready for crating.

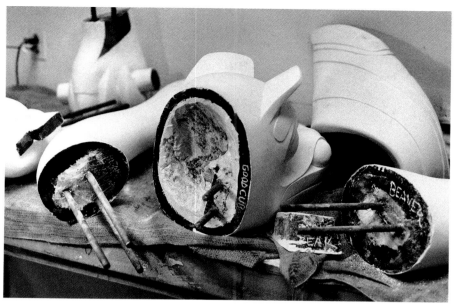

21 AUGUST 1989: At left, a few components of the plaster pattern, labeled and ready for crating.

23 OCTOBER 1989: Opposite page, the Ancient Reluctant Conscript, his face in its final form and his cedarbark cape nearly finished at last, sits alone in the hull, after all his fellow passengers have been dismembered and crated for shipment to the foundry.

15 NOVEMBER 1989: The finished components of the plaster pattern are loaded for shipment from Reid's studio in Vancouver to the Tallix Foundry in Beacon, New York.

25 NOVEMBER 1989: Three of Reid's crew – George Rammell, John Nutter and Nancy Brignall – uncrating and reassembling the plaster pattern at the foundry.

18 APRIL 1990: Don Yeomans carving the new yellowcedar pattern for the Chief's staff.

24 MAY 1990: Reid, working in red alder, carves a new pattern for the Killer Whale which will sit atop the staff. Two of his earlier sketches in paper and plaster are close at hand.

138

16 MAY 1990: Qaganjaat in her rubber and plaster cocoon. At the Tallix Foundry, Gerhard Gunter removes the sectioned plaster casing and the polyurethane rubber mold formed around Reid's original plaster pattern. The first layers of wax, meanwhile, are applied to the rubber mold of the Raven's tail.

16 MAY 1990: David Hyman and Kathy Wood peel the polysulfide rubber mold from the cast wax master of the Raven's head.

6 AUGUST 1990: The wax master of the Bad Cub, in his welded steel cage, is ready to begin the dipping process that will coat the wax with a hard ceramic shell.

6 AUGUST 1990: At the Tallix Foundry, Bill Kepler and John van Ambergh raise the dripping head of the Dogfish Woman from a vat of silica slurry. While still wet with the slurry, the head will be tumbled in a bed of zircon sand. When a sufficient thickness of silica has been built up in this way by repeated immersion in slurry and sand the mold will be heated in an autoclave to melt out the wax.

7 AUGUST 1990: Robert Holowiak and his coworkers, dressed in reflective asbestos, lower the hot ceramic mold of the Raven's tail into the sandpit. Behind them, Stephen Wood checks the temperature of the molten bronze.

7 AUGUST 1990: Molten bronze is poured simultaneously from two crucibles into the mouths of the half-buried ceramic mold, casting the Raven's tail.

On the same day, elsewhere in the Foundry, Ray Montadari is chasing the freshly cast bronze of the Bear Father's head.

21 JANUARY 1991: Reid with Dick Polich of the Tallix Foundry, discussing the positioning of the staff in the Chief's hand, and Polich guiding the staff into position.

22 JANUARY 1991: At left, the Ancient
Reluctant Conscript in raw, unpatinated
bronze.

Above, between the Eagle's eye and the
Bear Mother's cheek, the Chief is
clutching his staff.

7 MARCH 1991: The Conscript and the
Frog in their final incarnations as black
patinated bronze.

19 NOVEMBER 1991

160

The bibliography that follows this note is a list of suggestions for interested readers, not a reference list for scholars, but it includes the basic published sources. There is a full-scale bibliography in Suttles.

Most of my Haida quotations come from John Swanton's unpublished Haida manuscripts at the Library of the American Philosophical Society, Philadelphia. More information on Swanton, John Sky of the Qquuna Qiighawaai and Walter McGregor of the Qaayahllaanas can be found in my essay "That Also Is You: Some Classics of Native Canadian Literature."

The best of the Haida poets recorded by Swanton were speakers of the southern or Skidegate dialect, so I use that as a literary standard. Because I approach these texts as a poet and a classicist, not as a linguist or an anthropologist, I depart from standard linguistic practice and give preference to the oldest available solid evidence. Generally speaking, that means the pronunciations Swanton recorded in 1900–1901. I have also received brief but invaluable help from living speakers – in particular Mrs Florence Davidson of Masset – and abundant help and much generous advice – some of which, unhappily, I could not follow – from the linguist John Enrico.

It was Enrico who first alerted me to the difference between the archaic and current Haida names for Haida Gwaii. I've since been able to confirm this difference with Mrs Davidson.

*

I speak of classical or traditional Haida language, art and culture, not to imply that they were unchanging but to acknowledge clear evidence that they were healthier and more stable before the Haida holocaust than after. The cultural style of Northwest Coast mythological narrative is instantly recognizable, like the cultural style of the formline painting and carving. On closer inspection, the style of individual Haida mythtellers is just as perceptible as the style of individual visual artists. I take for granted that Haida oral literature has altered over time as much as Haida painting and sculpture. I also suspect that, in the genre of mythic narrative, it may have been equally tenacious of content and style.

Many structural and compositional features of Northwest Coast visual art have gone substantially unchanged for at least a thousand years. When I make deductions about "traditional" or "classical" Haida

Several systems exist for spelling Haida words, and I use a different system here than I've used in the past. Doubled vowels (aa, ii, uu) are long, and doubled consonants (gg, kk, ll, nn, qq, tt) are glottalized. Dl, hl and tl are laterals (λ, ł, ƛ). Ttl and tts are glottalized tl and ts. Ng is a velar nasal, as in the English singer. When the nasal is followed by a plosive, as in the English word English, I write ngg instead. When n and g are adjacent and distinct, as in the English name Wingate, I write them n-g. The apostrophe indicates a glottal stop; x is a velar fricative, like ch in German ich; q is a uvular k; gh and xh are uvular g and x.

In John Enrico's working orthography, which may become the standard, glottalized consonants are written with an apostrophe and uvulars with a superimposed hyphen. Thus Enrico writes q'adasgu qiigawaay where I prefer to write Qqadasghu Qiighawaai.

To complicate matters still further, I spell a few common phrases – e.g., Haida Gwaii and Gwaii Haanas – in the accepted popular way, though these spellings violate all of the systems.

For Tlingit names, I use the spelling system of Jeff Leer, which is revised from the standard orthography of Naish and Story.

thought from the works of nineteenth-century Haida poets, I base my inferences on features of the myths that seem to me analogous to the most persistent and durable features of the visual art. The corpus of Haida oral literature recorded at the end of the nineteenth century includes a number of autobiographical tales. These stories, like Haida portrait masks, have considerable room for realistic detail. Formline art does not. Reid describes it most succinctly, as a visual language in which "the line that defines the form *is* the form." There is no room in the system for the anecdotal truth of light and shadow or for naturalistic detail – which is part of the reason why there is no scale. The narratives of the mythtellers follow a similar rule. Like formline figures, the myths can be linked or intertwined, dismembered and redistributed, or nested one within the other, but they cannot be *expanded* by anecdotal incident or novelistic detail. Because they are no more realistic or naturalistic than formline art, they are useless as direct ethnological evidence. But they do pay close attention to the world. They are maps, not pictures, of reality.

*

I use the words *art, artist, poet, painting, sculpture* and *poetry* freely in relation to classical Haida culture. Sometimes I also use the word *philosophy*. It is true that I would be hard-pressed to translate some, but not all, of these terms back into Haida. I don't accept this as evidence that the things these words refer to didn't or don't exist in the Haida world. I have found no word for *art* per se in Haida. I have found no word for *formline* either. Still less are there terms for the constituent components of the northern formline system. There are also no names, so far as I know, for the parts of speech or the conjugations of the Haida verb. These things, it seems, were not discussed. But they were performed. If we choose to discuss them now, in English or in Haida, we will have to give them names.

Of course the connotations differ. *Painting*, in the art of the Northwest Coast, means a flat design, usually calligraphic and representational at the same time, applied to the surface of an object – usually an object meant to be used as well as looked at. Painting in this context rarely or never means an image made entirely of paint, on a surface whose only function is to hold the paint together. *Poetry* likewise never means something written and dated. I think it is better for us to remember that each of these words has a range of meanings, even within the confines of colonial and European history, than to pretend that, when we leave that history behind, phenomena like art, poetry and philosophy cease to exist.

Some scholars, and more importantly some Haida, may also object to

my calling some of the principal creatures of Haida mythology "gods."
The Haida word is *sghaana*, and I think the root meaning is something
like "power," in the superhuman sense. *Sghaana* is also the usual Haida
word for killer whale, but I take this as actually the abbreviated form of
sghaana ttigha, "animal of power." Most if not all Haida deities may at
their option assume the form of a killer whale, and this fact is crucial to
Haida cosmology, but I don't think the word is at root a species name.
Sghaana occurs in other compounds, such as *sghaanajaat*, "woman of
power," which I have often translated as goddess, and *sghaanaqiidas*,
"*sghaana*-born," which I translate, again, in certain contexts, as god or
gods. *Sghaa* is a shaman, and *sghaaghadas* means something like em-
powered or touched or inspired. The root may also be present in *sghaalt-
sit*, the Haida name for the northern flicker (*Colaptes auratus*) and
sghaalang, which is one of the words for song. *Sghan*, the red snapper
(*Sebastes spp.*), has a reputation for special potency as well, but I think
this is assonance instead of etymology.

In those contexts where it doesn't clearly mean killer whale, Swanton
translated *sghaana* as "supernatural being." Reid is not a Haida speaker,
but he knows the ground, and his usual English equivalent is
"mythcreature." Translating from Haida to Navajo, the terms that
come most readily to mind are *diyin dine'é* and *diyin daanilíinii*, which
converted in turn to English would be "holy people" and something like
"sacred beings." I don't see that "gods" is any less satisfactory as an
English synonym. "Immortals" won't do, though it may be logically
correct, because the gods of Haida Gwaii, the *sghaanaqiidas*, like all
things living, grow old, die and are reborn. Indeed, one of the obvious
Tsimshian translations is *yettsisgede*, which means literally "those who
are killed with a club"; the Kwakwala equivalent is *nuxhnemmise*. Boas
liked to render both these terms in English as "myth people," which is
not literal, but has much to commend it. Nevertheless, when a mythcreature or person who already possesses supranormal powers is further
translated into the landscape, the sea or the sky, as often happens at the
culmination of a Haida narrative poem, the word *sghaana* or one of its
compounds is used, and myth person or mythcreature is not a sufficient
translation. In Latin, one might say *numen* rather than *deus* – but I
notice that the lexicographer James Murray thought *numen*, not *deus*,
was the closest Latin equivalent to the English "god."

Death and old age, and alternate human and animal forms, are not
unknown to the gods of Europe and the Middle East, nor to the gods of
Asia and Oceania either. But in the mythworld of the northern Northwest Coast, the primary realm of the gods is not celestial, it is submarine. Perhaps it was so for some of the fishing and trading peoples of
pre-Olympian Greece as well. Disputes between Zeus and Poseidon are a

constant Homeric theme, and a large number of the older Greek divinities – Proteus, Nereus, Pontos, Doris, Thetis and Galatea, to name a few – reside beneath the sea. Hesiod wove dozens of their names into a genealogical pattern, but there is no fixed pantheon or census of these gods, either in Greece or in Haida Gwaii.

*

The summary of the Qqaaxhadajaat story recorded by Boas is in Swanton's *Haida Texts: Masset Dialect*, p 755. Edenshaw's remark on Qqaaxhadajaat and Nangdldastlas is recorded in Swanton's *Ethnology*, p 142. The Nangdldastlas story itself, told by John Sky, is in Swanton's *Haida Texts and Myths: Skidegate Dialect*, p 151f. Much else comes together in this complex, beautiful story of humans, divinities and a supernaturally gifted slave crossing the *xhaaidla* by canoe. This is, for instance, where Sky links Qaganjaat and Xaalajaat through marriage to human brothers, making the two fugitive, subterranean goddesses momentarily submarine sisters-in-law.

Taangghwanlaana, the One in the Sea, appears more often in the scholarly literature under some variant of his Tlingit name, Gunàkadèt. The northern Haida also adopted this name, along with other Tlingit terminology, sometime before 1900. In Tsimshian myths, Taangghwanlaana is called Nagunaks. Ttsaamuus, the Snag, crops up here and there in the literature in Swanton's spelling, as Tcamaos. In Shadbolt, the spelling used is Tschumos, which closely approximates Reid's preferred pronunciation. So far as I know, Boas is correct in tracing the Haida name to the Tsimshian *ttsimaks*, "in the water."

*

The Chilkat blanket worn by the Chief in the black canoe can be profitably compared with a Chilkat tunic, catalogue no. 11604, in the Crane Collection, Denver Museum of Natural History. Reid knows this tunic well, since it was formerly in the De Menil Collection and was published as item 60 in Reid & Holm, *Form and Freedom*. There are other tunics of similar design but varying size and workmanship – e.g., one in the Burke Museum, Seattle, and another in the Canadian Museum of Civilization.

*

The memorial pole that matches Xana's staff is Masset 10M2 in MacDonald's *Haida Monumental Art* (see plates 181, 183 & 185, pp 140–141). The story of Xana and Sigai is told in part by Margaret Blackman in *Syesis* 5 (1972), p 211f. (The Xana pictured in MacDonald, plates

182 & 201, is the disinherited nephew of Sigai and grandnephew of the Xana memorialized in the pole.)

The staff itself, which is full of other surprises and a great delight to hold, is mentioned briefly by Albert Niblack in the US National Museum Annual Report for 1888, *The Coast Indians of Southern Alaska and Northern British Columbia* (Washington, DC, 1890), but there is no information in Niblack not derived from the museum's curatorial record, and no information there that isn't dependent on the collector, James Swan. Swan identified the upper figures, unsatisfactorily, as "whale & crow," the lowest complete figure as "sparrowhawk *skamison*," and the incomplete figures at the bottom as "beaver eating mouse." *Skyaamskun* is Haida for falcon or hawk (including, I think, the sharp-shin, goshawk and peregrine), and this identification may be correct. Too little remains of the lower figures for me to identify them with certainty, but the larger face does not appear to be that of a Beaver, nor is there any visible confirmation that the smaller face belongs to a Mouse. The corresponding figures on Xana's pole are the snub-nosed or broken-beaked Raven, and the Bear with what is probably two cubs. The snub-nosed Raven on the pole matches the putative Hawk on the staff, but has human hands and a moon on the breast to confirm his identity, where the breast of the bird on the staff is plain.

The long-billed bird at the top of the pole and the staff can be confirmed as the Raven (rather than Cormorant or Heron) by comparing similar poles and by the architecture of the myths that lie behind them. The same combination of figures – transitional Raven above, Snag below – occurs profusely, especially on frontal poles. Readily visible examples include Chaatl pole 2, Haina 5, Kaisun 5, Masset 5 & 26, Ninstints 11, 12, 13 & 17, Skedans 13x & 182, Skidegate 20, Tanu 14 & 16 (all in MacDonald) and the two Skowal memorial poles at Kasaan (illustrated with Alan Hoover's pertinent essay in Abbott, *The World Is As Sharp As a Knife*, p 144). Note that Ninstints pole 11 is the rear pole in MacDonald's plate 144, and Ninstints 12 is the pole in plate 145, despite captions to the contrary. The round-eyed creature on the latter pole is the Frog. Reid's close acquaintance with some of these poles goes back to the 1957 salvage operations at Sghan-gwaai (Ninstints). He carved a duplicate of Ninstints 12 (see page 73) in 1959.

Since the story of the Raven and the Snag belongs to both sides, the creatures involved in it need not be taken as crests, but for heraldic reasons, Eagle families sometimes added an Eagle near the top or a Beaver near the bottom of the stack, or merely substituted the Beaver for the Seawolf or Sea Grizzly, which in this context is the usual form of the Snag. Very rarely, the Eagle displaces the Raven.

Other examples of the Raven in avian form with human fingers or hands include Ninstints pole 13, Skidegate 20, and the two Skowal poles at Kasaan. The fact that the fingers frequently *are* hands confirms that this is the Raven, and not, for instance, the Heron sucking his nails for knowledge (something which, in Haida myth, only the Heron and his allomorph Watghadagang seem to do).

Walter of the Sttlaangahlaanas told Swanton that Taangghwanlaana and Qiinggi were one in the same, thus confirming the congruence and mutability of the figures. But John Sky, a far more capable poet, preferred to portray the two as distinct. See Swanton, *Haida Texts: Masset Dialect*, pp 110–130 & 363.

Henry Moody's confirmation that the Snag's voice is equivalent to the Raven's is in Swanton's *Ethnology*, p 142. The Tlingit storyteller Dekinak'w makes the same point differently in his version of the broken beak episode. There, the fishermen who haul up the Raven's beak identify it as G̲unàkadèt's nose. See Swanton's *Tlingit Myths and Texts*, p 8.

John Sky's story of Quyaagyaaghandaal, which is not so simple as I have made it out to be, is published, with several related stories, in English in Swanton's *Haida Texts and Myths: Skidegate Dialect*, p 190.

Wilson Duff, in a brilliant performance shortly before his death, pointed out that the sex of the human in the raven rattle is not explicit. (See Duff, "The World Is As Sharp As a Knife: Meaning in Northern Northwest Coast Art," abridged in Abbott; full text in Carlson.) The absence of a labret proves nothing either way, since labrets are usually omitted in the art (as they may have been in life) when a tongue is shared. The Raven himself or herself is, of course, transsexual. Raven rattles were used, so far as I know, only by men, and in a society strongly divided on sexual lines. Perhaps those who used them had fixed opinions concerning the sex of the humans who trembled upside down on the backs of birds in their outstretched hands. To the best of my knowledge, no reliable tradition on these points has been preserved.

Items of particular importance for understanding Reid's work are marked with an asterisk.

* Abbott, Donald N., ed. *The World Is As Sharp As a Knife: An Anthology in Honour of Wilson Duff.* Victoria, BC: British Columbia Provincial Museum, 1981. [Includes important contributions by Reid, Wilson Duff, Bill Holm and others.]

Blackman, Margaret. *During My Time: Florence Edenshaw Davidson, A Haida Woman.* Seattle: University of Washington Press, 1982.

Boas, Franz. *Indianische Sagen von der Nord-Pazifischen Kuste Amerikas.* Berlin: Asher, 1895.

* ———. *Tsimshian Mythology.* BAE Ann. Rep. 31. Washington, DC: Bureau of American Ethnology, 1916. [Centred on the work of the Tsimshian writer Henry Tate, this is nevertheless the major comparative study of Northwest Coast mythology, including Haida, Tlingit and Kwakiutl as well as Tsimshian sources, and some others farther afield.]

Boddy, Trevor. "Erickson in Washington." *Canadian Architect* 34.7: pp 25-36. Toronto, 1989. [An analysis of the building for which *The Spirit of Haida Gwaii* was commissioned.]

* Bringhurst, Robert. "That Also Is You: Some Classics of Native Canadian Literature." *Canadian Literature* 124-5: pp 32-47. Vancouver, 1990. Reprinted in *Native Writers and Canadian Writing*, ed. W.H. New, Vancouver: University of British Columbia Press, 1990.

Carlson, Roy L., ed. *Indian Art Traditions of the Northwest Coast.* Burnaby, BC: Simon Fraser University, [1983]. [Useful especially for the prehistory of Northwest Coast art.]

Driver, Harold E. *Indians of North America.* Chicago: University of Chicago Press, 2nd ed., 1969. [The standard general text.]

Duff, Wilson, ed. *Arts of the Raven: Masterworks by the Northwest Coast Indians.* Exhibition Catalogue. Vancouver: Vancouver Art Gallery, 1967.

————. *Images: Stone: BC*. Exhibition Catalogue. Saanichton, BC: Hancock, 1975. [The only extensive study of Northwest Coast sculpture in stone.]

————. *The Indian History of British Columbia*, vol. 1: *The Impact of the White Man*. Victoria: Anthropology in British Columbia Memoir 5, 1964. [Unfortunately the only volume Duff completed of his projected Indian history.]

Emmons, George T. "The Chilkat Blanket." With notes by Franz Boas. *Memoirs of the American Museum of Natural History* III.4: pp 329-401. New York, 1907.

Erickson, Arthur. *The Architecture of Arthur Erickson*. Vancouver/Toronto: Douglas & McIntyre, 1988.

Fladmark, Knut. *British Columbia Prehistory*. Ottawa: National Museum of Man, 1986.

Holm, Bill. *The Box of Daylight: Northwest Coast Indian Art*. Seattle: Seattle Art Museum & University of Washington Press, 1983.

* ————. *Northwest Coast Indian Art: An Analysis of Form*. Seattle: University of Washington Press, 1965.

————. *Spirit and Ancestor*. Seattle: University of Washington Press, 1987. [A useful survey of coastal styles, from the Columbia River to Yakutat.]

Islands Protection Society. *Islands at the Edge: Preserving the Queen Charlotte Islands*. Vancouver/Toronto: Douglas & McIntyre, 1984. [Anthology focussing on the ecological richness of Haida Gwaii and the threat of industrial destruction.]

King, J.C.H. *Portrait Masks from the Northwest Coast of America*. London: Thames & Hudson, 1979.

Kroeber, A.L. *Cultural and Natural Areas of Native North America*. Berkeley: University of California Press, 1939.

Lévi-Strauss, Claude. *Anthropologie structurale*, 2 tomes, Paris: Plon, 1958 & 1973. Translated as *Structural Anthropology*, vol. 1, New York: Basic Books, 1963; vol. 2, Chicago: University of Chicago Press, 1976. [Vol. 1 contains the essay "Split Representation in the Art of Asia and America" and vol. 2, among other relevant items, "The Story of Asdiwal."]

————. "The Art of the Northwest Coast at the American Museum of Natural History." *Gazette des Beaux-Arts* 24: pp 175-82. Paris/New York, 1943.

———. *Des symboles et leurs doubles*. Paris: Plon, 1989. [This is for the most part an anthology culled from previous works, but it gives a convenient overview of Lévi-Strauss's writings on Native American art and on Bill Reid in particular.]

———. *La Voie des masques*. 2ème ed. Paris: Plon, 1979. Translated as *The Way of the Masks*. Seattle: University of Washington Press, 1982.

* MacDonald, George F. *Haida Monumental Art*. Vancouver: University of British Columbia Press, 1983. [Not without its errors and omissions, but this is the nearest thing to a full study of Haida "totem poles" as they existed at the end of the nineteenth century.]

Macnair, Peter L., & Alan L. Hoover. *The Magic Leaves: A History of Haida Argillite Carving*. Victoria: British Columbia Provincial Museum, 1984.

——— et al. *The Legacy: Tradition and Innovation in Northwest Coast Indian Art*. Vancouver/Toronto: Douglas & McIntyre, 1984.

Neich, Roger. "The Veil of Orthodoxy: Rotorua Ngati Tarawhai Woodcarving in a Changing Context." In Sidney M. Mead & Bernie Kernot, eds., *Art and Artists of Oceania*. Palmerston North, NZ: Dunmore, 1983. [An essay on post-contact Maori carving, relevant in many respects to post-contact Haida carving as well.]

* Reid, Bill. "These Shining Islands." In *Islands at the Edge*. [Perhaps the most eloquent of Reid's many pleas for saving Haida Gwaii from the ravages of large-scale clearcut logging.]

* ——— & Robert Bringhurst. *The Raven Steals the Light*. Vancouver/Toronto: Douglas & McIntyre; Seattle: University of Washington Press, 1984. Traduit comme *Le Dit du Corbeau*, Paris: Alpha Bleue, 1989.

* ——— & Bill Holm. *Form and Freedom: A Dialogue on Northwest Coast Indian Art*. Houston: Institute for the Arts, Rice University, 1975. Reissued [1978] as *Indian Art of the Northwest Coast: A Dialogue on Craftsmanship and Aesthetics*.

——— & Adelaide de Menil. *Out of the Silence*. New York: Harper & Row, 1971. [De Menil's photographs, with Reid's captions.]

Samuel, Cheryl. *The Chilkat Dancing Blanket*. Seattle: Pacific Search Press, 1982. Reissued, Norman: University of Oklahoma Press, 1989.

Schuster, Carl, & Edmund Carpenter. *Materials for the Study of Social Symbolism in Ancient and Tribal Art.* 3 vols in 12 parts. New York: Rock Foundation, 1986–88.

* Shadbolt, Doris. *Bill Reid.* Vancouver/Toronto: Douglas & McIntyre, 1986. [An excellent study of the artist and his work, current to the year in which the first clay sketches for *The Spirit of Haida Gwaii* were made.]

Suttles, Wayne, ed. *Handbook of North American Indians,* vol. 7: *Northwest Coast.* Washington, DC: Smithsonian Institution, 1990.

* Swanton, John R. *Contributions to the Ethnology of the Haida.* Publications of the Jesup North Pacific Expedition, vol. v.1. Leiden: E.J. Brill, 1905.

————. *Haida Texts: Masset Dialect.* Publications of the Jesup North Pacific Expedition, vol. x.2. Leiden: E.J. Brill, 1908.

* ————. *Haida Texts and Myths: Skidegate Dialect.* BAE Bull. 29. Washington, DC: Bureau of American Ethnology, 1905.

————. *Tlingit Myths and Texts.* BAE Bull. 39. Washington, DC: Bureau of American Ethnology, 1909.

Tennant, Paul. *Aboriginal Peoples and Politics: The Indian Land Question in British Columbia, 1849-1989.* Vancouver: University of British Columbia Press, 1990.

* Wardwell, Allen. *Objects of Bright Pride: Northwest Coast Indian Art from the American Museum of Natural History.* New York: Center for Inter-American Relations, 1978.

ACKNOWLEDGEMENTS

Brief as it is, this book was long in the making. Ulli Steltzer and I, together and separately, have been the beneficiaries of much help and kindness along the way.

George Rammell and all the crew who built *The Spirit of Haida Gwaii* were endlessly generous with information and helpful in countless other ways. So were Dick and Toni Polich and the staff at the Tallix Foundry, where the black canoe was cast. Joseph Miller gave us a desperately welcome refuge in New York City, full of music and good cheer — two essentials of serious thinking. Guujaaw of Skidegate, who appointed himself my editor, proved his skill in that difficult task many times.

John Enrico has taught me much about the Haida language, and I hope he'll forgive the fact that my spelling system continues to differ from his. I'm equally indebted to Bill Holm, though my interpretations of Haida iconography often differ from his as well. For help of many kinds, I'm thankful to Florence Davidson of Masset, Hugh Brody, Robert Davidson, Jeff Leer, William Sturtevant at the Smithsonian Institution, Dale Idiens at the Royal Scottish Museum, Leslie Mobbs at the National Archives in Ottawa, Andrea Lasala at the American Museum of Natural History, Terry Colli at the Canadian Embassy in Washington, and to Joff and Patricia Grohne of Bowen Island.

Books on subjects such as this are not produced in a world free of animosity and disagreement. Doris Shadbolt, her excellent study of Bill Reid, and Reid himself have all been welcome beacons in the storm.

I wrote the first full draft of this text in Scotland, as the pampered guest of the Scottish Arts Council through the Canada/Scotland literary exchange. It was difficult, under the circumstances, to ignore the similarities and the contagious interconnections between the fate of Gaelic-speaking Scots under English rule and the fate of Native Americans under regimes that are chiefly of British descent. I'm grateful to my Scottish hosts, and especially to Walter Cairns of the Scottish Arts Council, for their hospitality and their patience with my distress during that time.

Finally and primarily, we are grateful to Bill Reid.

R.B.

TECHNICAL SUMMARY

Artist:	Bill Reid (1920–)
Title:	*The Spirit of Haida Gwaii*
Date:	modelling begun 1986; plaster pattern completed 1989; casting completed 1991
Material:	Cast bronze with black patina
Length:	605 cm (19′10″)
Height:	389 cm (12′9″)
Width:	348 cm (11′5″)
Weight:	4900 kg (10,800 lb)
Hull:	LOA, 564 cm (18′6″); beam, 193 cm (6′4″); freeboard, 80 cm (2′7″)
Foundry:	Tallix Foundry, Beacon, New York
Location:	Canadian Chancery, Washington, DC Plaster pattern in the Canadian Museum of Civilization, Ottawa
Owner:	Government of Canada, funded by Nabisco Brands Canada

The text of this book is set in Aldus roman and italic, designed by Hermann Zapf. The titling face is Lithos, designed by Carol Twombly. The book was designed by Robert Bringhurst, nurtured and fed by Ulli Steltzer, and set into type by The Typeworks, Vancouver. The paper is Leykam, made in Austria. Both the text and the photographs were printed by C.S. Graphics, Singapore.